# THE LOVE OF ETERNAL WISDOM

**THE FOLLOWING OF CHRIST**—"Anyone who wishes to follow Me must deny himself, take up his cross, and follow Me" (Mk 8:34).

# THE LOVE OF ETERNAL WISDOM

with
Reading Guide

by

Saint Louis-Marie
Grignion de Montfort

Catholic Book Publishing Corp.
New Jersey

NIHIL OBSTAT: Rev. Pawel Tomczyk, Ph.D.
Censor Librorum

IMPRIMATUR: ✠ Kevin J. Sweeney, D.D.
Bishop of Paterson

August 21, 2023

The Nihil Obstat and Imprimatur are official declarations that a book or a pamphlet is free of doctrinal or moral error. No implication is contained therein that those who have granted the Nihil Obstat and Imprimatur agree with the contents, opinions, or statements expressed.

This book was originally published in French © Medisaspaul Editions, 48 rue du Four, 76006 Paris, France.



(T-323)

ISBN 978-1-953152-99-2



Printed in China 23 HH 1

catholicbookpublishing.com

# CONTENTS

## Explanation of the Painting

(Work of G. Pranovi—1964)

According to tradition, Montfort wrote *The Love of Eternal Wisdom* during the second half of 1703. He was living in great hardship. Dismissed from the General Hospital of Poitiers as well as from La Salpêtrière in Paris three years after his ordination, he found himself without work, without future, without support. He took refuge under a staircase in rue du Pot-de-Fer in Paris. The artist wanted to express his total stripping: barefoot, small empty bowl. Montfort transformed this poverty into a burning desire for Christ, eternal and incarnate Wisdom. Guided by the Virgin Mary, in the light of the cross, he had an intense mystical experience. His traveling bag was hanging on the wall: he would take it with him as he travelled the roads of the west of France, to light up this love for Christ in the hearts of the people.

# Introduction

*This book is like a letter from a lover to her beloved, to win her affection* (LEW 65).

*The Love of Eternal Wisdom*, written by Saint Louis-Marie Grignion de Montfort in 1703-1704, is a major work that presents us with the entire Montfortian spirituality. It reveals the source, the passion and the dynamism that had guided his deep relationship with God, his missionary commitment, and the path of his conversion.

In *The Love of Eternal Wisdom*, Montfort offered people of all ages who are driven by the desire to find meaning in their lives, a wisdom of being and living that leads to true happiness. For this great missionary and mystic had grasped, in the very heart of his human experience, nourished and enlightened by the Wisdom books, that Wisdom reveals her love to us in the heart of our human and global realities.

In the first part of this work, Montfort took the time to describe the beauty and qualities of Eternal Wisdom "in eternity, where she dwells in the bosom of the Father, in the dimension of time shining forth in the creation of the cosmos, in her incarnation and glorious and triumphant in the heavens" (LEW 14). But more than any thing, he wanted to present her as the lover in search of her beloved—that is, every human being—to show the incredible love she has for each one. *My delight, says Wisdom, is to be with the children of humanity* (Prov 8:31).

The life of Montfort would be completely upended and transformed by this lover's desire for Wisdom bound so closely to the existence of human beings to the point of becoming man in Jesus and wanting to live fully all the stages of our existence.

This is why the Incarnation is the central mystery of all the spirituality and life of Montfort. In his missions, in his writings and through all his initiatives, he would, like Wisdom, proclaim this love to everyone he met and especially to the most deprived. Always, he wants to demonstrate the qualities of the love he had discovered in eternal and incarnate Wisdom.

Montfort showed that, preceding human beings in everything, Wisdom takes the initiative and goes in search of their hearts:

> At times she seeks humans on the highways and byways; at other times she climbs the mountain peaks; sometimes she comes to the city gates; or else she enters the marketplaces or the courts, crying out as loudly as possible:

> O you humans, you children of humankind! It is you I have been calling for so long! To you I lift my voice; you are my desire; it is you I seek; it is you whom I claim for my own. Listen and come to me; I want to make you happy (LEW 66).

The love of Wisdom described by Montfort wanted to arouse our love. Also, in the second part of his work, Montfort invited us to meet Wisdom in contemplation. It is only by allowing oneself to be touched by her love that the desire to search for, to know and to possess her will awaken in us.

> Is it possible to love what one does not know? Can one love passionately what one knows only imperfectly? How can it be that people have so little love for the incomparable Jesus—Eternal and Incarnate Wisdom—unless it is because they do not know Wisdom herself, or know her so very little? (LEW 8).

Knowing and loving are intimately linked, because to love the other is to be born with the other to new life. This is what the numerous passages in the Bible's Wisdom books suggest to us, which Montfort presents for our meditation throughout *The Love of Eternal Wisdom*, a true *lectio divina* of the Wisdom Books.

Both in the Old and the New Testament, where, in the person of Christ, she is even going to take on the dimension of time and flesh with us, Wisdom wishes to propose to the human being to know her to discover in her a path of happiness, a way of life.

Drawing on his own experience, Montfort concludes his work by presenting us with four concrete means to acquire Wisdom, as gifts that she offers us to respond to her proposal of love.

Always, the persons who are marked as wise, show that they have acquired the art of doing, directing, speaking, living by exercising a deep and contemplative listening to Creation, other human beings and themselves.

In his work, Montfort echoes a long tradition of biblical wisdom learned and described by human beings from diverse cultures who, over the centuries, have come into contact with each other to share their experience of God. Since then, Montfort and many others have recognized in Jesus *the power and the wisdom of God* (1 Cor 1:24).

We are immersed in a complex and disconcerting world, in search of true relationships, but often diluted in a virtual and passing world that disappoints. This is a world where hands are extended towards each other through humanitarian projects, yet at the same time where walls are erected through fear of the other. This is a world where money and not the dignity of the human being dictates our so-called democratic decisions. Yes: this world, our world, appears to us breathless in its quest for a compass that can direct it to what is true, to what is essential. Our world needs wisdom and wise people.

Throughout the sometimes unexpected pages of this work, Montfort offers us a reading imbued with divine wisdom which still responds today to the long and obscure search of men and women seeking a spiritual path that will lead them to true happiness and give meaning to their lives.

*Sr. Louise Madore, fdls, Congregational Leader*

**Note on the Presentation of the New Edition of *The Love of Eternal Wisdom***

## 1. Biblical Quotations

According to Maurice Gilbert SJ, no book of spirituality of this period contains so many biblical quotations from the Book of Wisdom and the main biblical Wisdom writings (Proverbs and Sirach)! Sometimes Montfort quotes whole chapters. Sometimes he inserts words, names, to clarify the meaning. Sometimes he seems to quote from memory because, while keeping the meaning of the passage, he does not quote it as it is. Here is how we proceeded:

1.1 From the manuscript, we compared the quotations from Montfort to the text of the Bible by Lemaîstre de Sacy (complete edition of 1696), the Bible used by Montfort. Generally, we respected the Montfort text, while completing or correcting it if necessary, from Lemaîstre de Sacy. We have also consulted the text published in the *Complete Works* (Threshold, 1966).

1.2 Biblical quotations exceeding three lines were indented, without quotation marks. The shorter passages were enclosed in quotation marks, followed by the reference in parentheses and in a smaller font. The numbers of verses were shown, as in the modern editions of the Bible. It should be noted that the French translation of Lemaîstre de Sacy is based largely on the Vulgate (Latin translation of Saint Jerome) and not on the manuscripts in the original languages (Hebrew and Greek), as for our modern Bibles. The text can be different; moreover, the numbering of the verses of Lemaîstre de Sacy does not always correspond to that of our modern Bibles.

1.3. The biblical texts are in italics and the words inserted by Montfort are in roman character.

## 2. Punctuation

The manuscript has only minimal punctuation: periods, a few commas, few paragraphs, some numbering. So we added punctuation marks to make reading and comprehension easier.

## 3. The Notes

This edition is intended for the general public. We have reduced the footnotes to author references, or to indicate a biblical passage whose text inspired Montfort. Some notes have been added to clarify the meaning of some passages.

## 4. The Canticles

Already the 1932 standard edition contained some hymns of Montfort in the appendix. We have chosen a few that are like a lyrical resonance of Montfort's text. They are placed at the end of the chapters whose theme they repeat. For those reproduced in this edition, we have followed the text of the *Complete Works*.

*Georges Madore, smm*

## Prayer to Eternal Wisdom

**1. O Divine Wisdom, Queen of Heaven and Earth, bowing humbly before you[1], I beg you in your graciousness to forgive the way I have so boldly taken it upon myself to speak of your greatness, for I am ignorant and unworthy. I pray you, look not upon the darkness of my mind, nor the clumsiness of my speech. If you do look upon these things, let it be with a kind and forgiving eye, and a gentle breath from your mouth. You, who are absolutely radiant with beauty and sweetness, have saved me from so many misfortunes and have filled my cup with so many blessings. Yet you remain unknown and even scorned by most people. So how could I keep silent about you? Not only do justice and gratitude command me to speak, but even my own self-interest urges me to do so even though I feel I can only babble like a small child. In a way I am only a child: and by speaking childishly, I hope to learn to speak more skilfully, until I have reached the *full maturity of your discipleship* (Eph 4:13).**

**2. I must confess that it almost seems to me that there is no clarity or order in what I am writing[2], but because my desire to possess you is so**

---

1 These first words are inspired by the Prayer of Solomon. Like the wise person of the Bible, Montfort addresses himself to the Creator God (Ws 9: 9) and makes an act of humility. (Ws 9: 4-6, 13, 17).

2 As in his other writings, Montfort does not lack order or method in this work. See the outline of his presentation at nos. 7 and 14.

great like Solomon, *I feel driven to turn impulsively in every direction as I seek you.* (Ws 8:18). If I dare to concentrate my efforts on making you known in this world, it is because you yourself have promised that *all who explain you and make you understood will have eternal life* (Si 24:31). Accept then, my gracious Princess, these first clumsy words about you as if they were already expressed in elegant language. Receive the strokes of my pen as though they were ordered steps on the path I take to find you. And *from the power of your throne* (Ws 9:4, 10), grant me the blessings and the light to represent you in such a way that all who listen will burn anew with the desire to love you and to possess you in this life and in eternity.

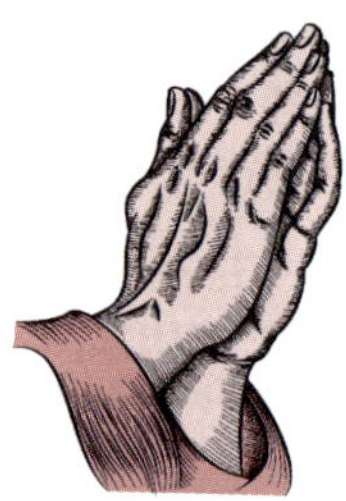

## Preliminary advice that wisdom gives to the rulers and great ones of the world in the sixth chapter of *the Book of Wisdom*[1]

**3.** [1] *Wisdom is greater than strength, and the prudent person is worthier than the courageous one.* [2] *Listen then, kings, and understand; receive instruction, judges of the world.* [3] *Hear this, you who govern great populations, taking pride in your hosts of subject nations!* [4] *Remember that you have received this power from the Lord, this dominion from the Most High; He will test your works and probe the depths of your thoughts.* [5] *If therefore, as servants of his kingdom, you have not ruled justly, nor observed the law, nor followed the will of God...* [6] *He will fall on you terribly and in a short time. Because on those in high places a ruthless judgment falls.* [7] *The lowly are pardoned more easily, out of pity but the mighty will be mightily tormented.* [8] *For the Lord of all does not shiver in fear before anyone; he does not stand in awe of greatness since he himself has made small and great and provides for all alike.* [9] *But the mighty will be more mightily tormented.* [10] *So rulers of*

1 Montfort fully quotes Wis 6:1-27; verses 1-10 are a real diatribe against the great and powerful who have failed to govern with wisdom and justice. On the other hand, verses 11-27 present a pressing exhortation to seek wisdom and justice. Montfort's commentary will be brief; no. 5 will cover the second part of the biblical text, and no. 6 will cover the first.

*kingdoms, my words are meant for you so that you may learn wisdom and not fall into error.* [11] *For those who in justice observe holy things will be adjudged just and accepting instruction from my words will find in them their defense.* [12] *Set your heart, therefore, on what I have to say, love my words, and you will be instructed.*

**4.** [13] *Wisdom is brilliant; she never fades. By those who love her, she is easily seen; by those who seek her, she is easily found.* [14] *She anticipates those who desire her by first making herself known.* [15] *Whoever gets up early to seek her will have no trouble, but will find her standing at the door.* [16] *Meditating on her is prudence in its perfect form, and anyone keeping awake for her will soon be free from care.* [17] *For she herself searches everywhere for those who are worthy of her, with kind good will she appears to them on their ways, knowing beforehand their every thought.*[18] *For Wisdom begins with the sincere desire for instruction.* [19] *Eagerness for instruction means loving her; attention to her laws guarantees perfect purity.* [20] *And perfect purity brings us near to God.* [21] *The desire for Wisdom thus leads to sovereignty the kingdom everlasting.* [22] *If then thrones and ruling rods delight you, kings and queens of the nations, honor Wis-*

*dom, so that you may reign forever.* 23 *Love*
*the light of Wisdom, all you who command*
*the peoples of the world.* 24 *What Wisdom is,*
*and how she was born, I shall now explain;*
*I shall hide no mysteries from you but shall*
*follow her steps from the outset of her ori-*
*gin, setting out what we know of her in full*
*light without departing from the truth.* 25 *De-*
*structive envy is not the companion for me,*
*for envy has nothing in common with Wis-*
*dom.* 26 *In the greatest number of wise men*
*lies the world's salvation, in a wise king re-*
*sides the stability of a people.* 27 *Learn there-*
*fore from my words; the gain will be yours.*

**5.** I have not wished, dear reader, to mix my own feeble words with the authoritative words of the Holy Spirit in this chapter. But please permit me to make a few observations.

1) How sweet is Eternal Wisdom in herself, how easy to approach and how attractive—even though she is so brilliant, so excellent, and so exalted! She calls to human beings in order to teach them the ways of happiness; she seeks them; she smiles upon them; she fills them with blessings; she knows their desires beforehand and hastens to fulfil them in a thousand ways, even to the point of sitting at their doorstep and waiting for them, to offer them the tokens of her affection. Could anyone have a heart and refuse it to her who conquers all hearts?

6. 2) What misfortune befalls the powerful and the rich when they do not love Wisdom! The words she addresses to them are terrifying! Our language is inadequate to express these warnings:

> "Suddenly and terribly (God) will appear to you... a most severe judgment will come upon those who preside over others... the powerful will be powerfully punished, and the most powerful will undergo the greatest torments" (Ws 6:6, 7, 9).

To these words we can add some that Wisdom spoke herself or through the scriptures after her Incarnation: "*Woe to you rich,*" *(Lk 6:24)* "*For it is easier for a camel to get through the eye of a needle than for a rich person to enter the kingdom of heaven*" (Mt 9:24, Mk 10:25, Lk 18:25).

These words were so often spoken by Divine Wisdom while she lived on earth, that three evangelists reported them in exactly the same way without changing anything—which ought to make the rich of this world either dissolve into tears or cry out in terror. "*Weep O rich ones, weep over the miseries that are about to befall you*" (Jas 5:1). Alas, however, these people have had their reward; they seem to live slavishly under the spell of their pleasures and riches that they do not see the dreadful consequences that are hanging over their heads.

**7.** 3) Solomon pledges his word that he is handing down a faithful and exact portrait of Wisdom; and that neither envy nor pride—both of which are the opposite of love—will prevent him from communicating the science that was given him from above. So he is not concerned that others might equal or surpass him in knowledge.[2]

I propose to follow the example of this great sage in unfolding to you who Wisdom is before her Incarnation, during her Incarnation, since her Incarnation and the means to obtain her and to keep her. Lacking, however, the abundance of knowledge and the enlightenment of Solomon, it is not pride and envy that I must fear, so much as my own poor abilities and ignorance. I beg you, in your charity, to overlook and excuse these shortcomings.

2 Cf. Ws 6:24-26

# Chapter 1

## To Love and Seek After Divine Wisdom It Is Necessary to Know Her

8. IS IT possible to love what one does not know? Can one love passionately what one knows only imperfectly? How can it be that people have so little love for the incomparable Jesus—Eternal and Incarnate Wisdom—unless it is because they do not know Wisdom herself, or know her[1] so very little? There is hardly anyone who studies properly—like St. Paul—the 'supreme science' of Jesus,[2] which is the noblest, the most satisfying, the most useful, and the most necessary of all the 'sciences' and forms of 'knowledge' that exist, in heaven or on earth.

9. 1) First of all it is the noblest of all the sciences, because its object is Wisdom, Uncreated and Incarnate, who is so splendid and highly exalted in the reality of her nature. She encompasses in herself the *fullness of divinity* (Col 2:9) and of humanity. In her is all that is greatest in heaven and on earth: all creatures visible and invisible, spiritual and material. St. John Chrysostom has said that Our Lord contains within himself a perfect summary of the

1 When speaking of Eternal and Incarnate Wisdom or Jesus Christ, Montfort refers to the same person. That is why in the following phrases he uses masculine or feminine pronouns to show this.

2 Cf. Eph 3:19

works of God; he is a perfectly focused image of all the perfections of God as well as those of all created beings. "Jesus Christ, Eternal Wisdom, is all that you can and ought to desire. Desire him; seek him; for he is the unique and precious pearl[3] for which you should not hesitate to sell all that you have." "*Let not the expert boast of wisdom, nor the hero of strength, nor the rich person of wealth;*" but "*Let anyone who glories do so in knowing me, and not in knowing anything else*" (Jer 9:23-24).

**10.** 2) There is nothing as soul-satisfying as the knowledge of Divine Wisdom; happy those who listen to her; happier still are those who desire her and seek her; but happiest of all are those who keep her ways,[4] and taste in their hearts the infinite sweetness that is the delight of the Eternal Father and the glory of the angels. If we could know the sweetness tasted by a soul who has experienced the beauty of Wisdom, enjoyed by a soul who is nourished with milk from this 'breast of the Father' we would exclaim with the Spouse of the Canticle, "*The milk of your breast is sweeter than wine,*" (Cant 1:1; 4:10) and more delightful than all the comforts of this world. Especially would we know it in those moments of contemplation when we are given to hear Wisdom's words: "*Taste and see;*"

3 Cf. Mt 13:43-44

4 Cf. Pr 8:32-34

(Ps 33:8) "*Eat and drink*" (Pr 9:5; Is 55:11) with my inexhaustible sweetness, "*for my conversation has nothing disagreeable in it, nor has my company anything tiresome in it; in my company you will find only satisfaction and joy*" (Ws 8:16).

**11.** 1) Knowing Eternal Wisdom is not only the noblest and the sweetest knowledge; it is also the most useful and necessary, because "eternal life consists in this—to know God and his Son Jesus Christ." "*To know you*"—exclaims the sage—"*is to know perfect justice. And to understand your fair judgments and your power is the root of immortality*" (Ws 15:3). If we truly wish to have eternal life, let us become acquainted with Eternal Wisdom; if we wish to have the perfection of holiness in this world, let us become familiar with Wisdom. If we want to have the root of immortality in our heart, let us have in our mind the intimate knowledge of Wisdom. To know Jesus Christ,[5] Wisdom Incarnate is to know enough. To know everything else and not know him is to know nothing.

**12.** What use is it to an archer to know how to shoot in the general direction of his target, if he doesn't know how to aim right into the bull's-eye? What good is it to us to know other sciences that may be necessary for our salvation if we don't know the science of Jesus Christ,

5 Cf. Jn 17:3

which is the most necessary, and indeed in the end is the centerpoint towards which everything else must converge? Although he possessed great knowledge in many areas and was very skilled in the literary arts of his time, the Apostle Paul confessed that he felt he knew nothing except Jesus Christ crucified. "I was resolved that the only knowledge I would have while I was with you was knowledge of Jesus and of him as the crucified Christ" (1Cor 2:2). With him let us say:

> *But what were once my assets I now, through Christ Jesus, count as losses. Yes, I will go further: because of the supreme advantage of knowing Christ Jesus my Lord. I count everything else as a loss.*

Now I see and know by experience that this knowledge is so excellent, so soul-satisfying, noble, useful and admirable to me that I no longer take an interest in anything else I have learned. All that once was so fascinating to me seems now trivial or foolish, so that it feels like a waste of time to take pleasure in my former pursuits.

> *"I say this to make sure that no one deceives you with false arguments. I assure you that Jesus Christ is the wellspring of all knowledge.* So make sure that no one deceives you with the empty attraction of a 'philos-

ophy' of the kind that human beings pass on, based on the principles of the world and not of Christ" (Col 2:4, 8). Continue to grow in the grace and knowledge of our Lord and Savior Jesus Christ. To this end, we are going to develop the subject of this knowledge in the succeeding chapters. But first let us make some distinctions between the various kinds of wisdom.

**13.** Wisdom in the general sense—as the root of the word itself reveals—is "knowledge to be tasted at length and with delight." In other words, it refers to a 'taste' for God and for divine truth.[6] Among the various classifications of wisdom, we must first make the distinction between true wisdom and its false imitation. True wisdom is the taste for the bare truth, stripped of lies and deceptions. False wisdom, on the other hand, is the taste for lies that are disguised under the appearance of truth. This false wisdom is the wisdom of worldly strategies which the Holy Spirit divides into three categories: earthly wisdom, sensual (animal) wisdom, and diabolical wisdom (Jas 3:15). True wisdom can be classified as either natural or supernat-

6 Here Montfort retakes a Latin expression of Wisdom largely used by spiritual authors and theologians of the Middle Ages. In Latin the etymological link between sapiential and *sapida* is undeniable. Wisdom is well and good a "tasty" science, that is to say that Wisdom is to know and to savor. The reading guide presents an explanation of the sense of Wisdom in the Bible and the orientation given by Montfort.

ural. Natural wisdom is the supreme knowledge of nature in its root principles and deep sources. Supernatural wisdom is the knowledge of things that are supernatural and divine in their origin. This supernatural wisdom can be further divided into the Wisdom that is substantial and uncreated, and wisdom that is accidental and created. Created wisdom is Uncreated Wisdom's self-communication—thus it is called the gift of wisdom. Substantial, uncreated Wisdom is the Son of God, the second Person of the Blessed Trinity; in other words, Eternal Wisdom in eternity, or Jesus Christ in the dimension of time. It is of this Wisdom that we shall be speaking.

**14.** We shall speak first of her origin contemplating her in eternity, where she dwells in the bosom of the Father as the object of divine contemplation and delight.

- Then we shall see her in the dimension of time shining forth in the creation of the cosmos.
- We shall go on to observe her in her humbled, incarnate condition in her life as a mortal human being.
- And finally, we shall meet her glorious and triumphant in the heavens.

- We shall end by surveying the means that we must learn to use in order to attain and keep Wisdom.

I leave to the philosophers their arguments, which I count as useless; I leave to the alchemists the secrets of their worldly wisdom. "But still to those who have reached maturity, we do not talk of Wisdom nor, it is true, a philosophy of this age or of the riches of this age, which will not last long now" (1 Cor 2:6). We shall speak, then, of true Wisdom, Eternal Wisdom Uncreated and Incarnate; and we shall direct our words to the 'perfect souls'—the elect.

## In Search of Wisdom

(Canticle 125:2, 6-9)

Then let us all seek Wisdom,
she is a hidden treasure
We must seek her constantly,
nothing should restrain us.
Let us roam around the worlds,
the heavens, the earth and seas
Suffering, sparing nothing,
so this wealth may be found.

Let us knock at the door
of a most Gracious God
He himself exhorts us to fear not pester Him.
We must repeat our needs,
increase our sufferings
And in holy rapture shout even the louder.

O Divine Mary, you alone have found
Incarnate Wisdom in the Word enfleshed.
Being His great Mistress, love now impels you
To send Him to us, to teach us all,
To help us all, to help us all.

O Divine Wisdom, Source of truth itself,
The world forsakes you, following vanity.
We will all seek you, with most lively faith
And no matter what, Yourself,
we beg reveal. (*twice*)

O Wisdom assistant of the Divinity!
We eagerly await your beauty to behold.
Having designed this promise,
why then delay so long
This gift so glorious? O come,
o come at last! (*twice*)

## Chapter 2

### Eternal Wisdom's Origin and Excellence[1]

15. AT THIS point one is compelled to exclaim with St. Paul: "*How deep, how immense is the Wisdom of God!*" (Rm 11:33). "*What angel is sufficiently enlightened and what human being is sufficiently daring to volunteer to explain Wisdom's origin to us?*" (Is 55:8; Ac 8:33). Faced with such a challenge, we can only close our eyes for fear of being overwhelmed by so brilliant and so vibrant a light! We can only hold our tongues for fear of spoiling so perfect a beauty by our very desire to speak about it. We can only keep silent and adore lest we be crushed by the immense glory of the very mystery we seek to penetrate.

16. Nevertheless we are given an idea of her in the Book of Wisdom, which the Holy Spirit composed just for our sake in order to accommodate our limitations.

> *Eternal Wisdom is a breath of the power of God, a pure outpouring of the glory of the*

1 In this chapter the author begins his presentation on Wisdom "from her origin ... in eternity, residing in the womb of her Father, as the object of his indulgence" (no. 14); it is this personal relationship of Wisdom with the Eternal Father that constitutes her excellence. And this excellence will be the first in a series of motifs that Montfort will enumerate as the foundations of love, research and the possession of Wisdom; cf. no. 181: "her origin, her beauty, her treasures, her desires"; no. 195: "her person, her treasures and her alliance."

*Almighty; so nothing impure can find its way into her. She is a reflection of the eternal light, unspotted mirror of God's active power, and the image of his goodness* (Ws 7:25-26).

**17.** This genuine and eternal idea of the divine beauty was revealed to St. John the Evangelist in the inexpressible joy that came upon him on the island of Patmos, when he was moved to exclaim: "*In the beginning was the Word,* or the Son of God, Eternal Wisdom *and the Word was in God, and the Word was God*" (Jn 1:1).

**18.** There are several places in the writings of Solomon[2] where it is said that Wisdom was created, that is, brought forth from the beginning, before all things and before all ages. She says of herself: "*From everlasting, I was firmly set, from the beginning, before the earth came into being and before the deep abyss existed, I was born*" (Pr 8:23-24).

**19.** In the supreme beauty of Wisdom, God the Father took his delight, in eternity and in time, as he himself gave witness at the time of the Baptism and the Transfiguration of Wisdom Incarnate: "*This is my beloved Son, in whom I am well pleased*" (Mt 3:17; 2 Pet 1:17). Of her shining and incomprehensible brightness, the Apos-

2 Si 1:4, 9; 24:14; Pr 8: 22 (according to Greek and Hebrew). "The writings of Solomon" refers to all the wisdom books of the Old Testament.

tles at the transfiguration saw but a few rays—a brief and incomplete perception which, nevertheless, filled them with consolation and ecstasy,

"Of immense splendor is Eternal Wisdom vast,
sublime, everlasting, more ancient than
the created universe."[3]

I myself have no words to express my idea of this beauty, this essence of all sweetness; but though my own idea is totally inadequate to express her excellence, who, in fact, might there be who has a clear idea of her and is able to explain it properly? Only you, O God, have this knowledge, and can communicate it to whomever you choose.

**20.** What follows is the way Wisdom herself speaks about who she is, through the effects she produces in souls. I will not mix my own words with hers, because I do not wish to reduce the splendor and magnificence that is hers. I refer you then to Ecclesiasticus (Sirach) chapter 24.

[1] *"Wisdom speaks her own praises; in the midst of her people she glories in herself.* [2] *She opens her mouth in the assembly of the Most High; she glories in herself in the presence of the Mighty One. She will be raised high in the midst of her people, and she will be admired in the*

3 Latin hymn of Vespers for the feast of the Transfiguration v. 2.

*assembly of the holy ones. She will receive praises amongst the multitude of the elect, and she will be blessed by those who are blessed by God. She will say:*

**21.** [3a] *I came forth from the mouth of the Most High; I was born before all creatures.*
[3b] *I gave birth in the heavens to a great light that shall never be extinguished and I covered the earth like a mist.* [4] *My dwelling place was in the heights, and my throne was a pillar of cloud.*
[5] *Alone, I have made the rounds of the heavens and walked through the depths of the abyss.*
[6] *Over the waves of the sea and over the whole earth, and over every people and nation I have held sway.*

**22.** [7] *By my power I established dominion over the hearts of all people, both the great and the lowly: among all these I searched for rest, and looked to see in whose territory I might pitch camp.*

**23.** [8a] *Then the Creator of all things instructed me; and he who created me fixed a place for my tent.* [8b] *He said, pitch your tent in Jacob; make Israel your inheritance, and take root in my elect.*

**24.** [9] *From eternity, in the beginning, He created me, and for eternity I shall remain.* [10] *In the holy tent I ministered before Him, and thus be-*

*came established in Zion.* [11] *In the beloved city He has given me rest, and in Jerusalem I exercise my authority.*

**25.** [12] *I have taken root in a privileged people, in the Lord's property, in His inheritance.* [13] *I have grown as tall as a cedar on Lebanon, as a cypress on Mount Hermon; I have grown as tall as a palm in En-Gedi, as the rose bushes of Jericho, as a fine olive in the plain, as a plane tree, I have grown tall.* [15a] *Like cinnamon and acanthus, I have yielded a perfume; like choice myrrh, I have breathed out a scent;* [15b] *like galbanum, onycha, labdanum, [a perfume box], like smoke of incense in the tent; and my fragrance is like that of purest balm.* [16] *I spread my branches like a terebinth, and my branches are glorious and graceful.* [17] *I am like a vine putting out graceful shoots, my blossoms bear the fruit of glory and wealth.*

**26.** [18] I am the mother of fair love, of fear, of knowledge, and of holy hope. *In me is all grace of the way and of the truth; in me is all hope of life and of virtue.*

**27.** [19] *Approach me you who desire me, and take your fill of my fruits, for memories of me are sweeter than honey; inheriting me is sweeter than the honeycomb. The memory of my name will be passed on through all ages.*

**28.** [21] They who eat me will hunger for more; they who drink me will thirst for more. [22] *No one who obeys me will ever have to blush; no one who acts as I dictate will ever sin.* [23] *All this is no other than the Book of the Covenant of the Most High and the knowledge of the truth."*

**29.** Wisdom compares herself to a great variety of these trees and plants—all of which bear different fruits and display different qualities. These images point to the great variety of states, functions and virtues that may mark human souls.

Such souls may appear like:

- cedars by the movement of their hearts towards the highest heavens;
- cypresses by their steadfast meditation on death;
- palm trees by their humble endurance of difficult labor;
- rose bushes by their vocation to martyrdom or the shedding of blood;
- plane trees that grow along the banks of flowing rivers;
- or terebinths with wide-spreading branches which recall their all-embracing charity towards the community.

Then there are all the other fragrant plants—balm, myrrh, etc.—that are less exposed to view. These are like hidden souls whose desire is to be known above all to God rather than to other human beings.

**30.** Having revealed herself as the mother and the source of all that is desirable, Wisdom urgently invites all humans to leave everything in order to desire her alone; for, as St. Augustine says, she gives herself only to those who desire and seek her with all the passion and commitment that such a great favor deserves. In the last verses of Sirach 24 quoted above, Wisdom notes three degrees of devotion, the last of which is its perfection:

1. to listen to God in humility and surrender to him,

2. to act in him and through him with faithful perseverance,

3. and finally, to seek to attain the necessary light and unction, to be able to inspire others to love Wisdom, so that they too may be guided to eternal life.

## Prayers to Wisdom

(Canticle 126:1, 3, 9)

O Divine Wisdom, I love you ardently!
You are my mistress, I am your lover!
On earth you alone I seek and I love;
You are so attractive,
I am just about delirious!

Where is your dwelling?
Wisdom let me know.
I will fly there right now;
love orders me to do so.
Must I cross the seas and roam
through the world?
Must I soar through the air?
Anything to find you.

O Eternal Wisdom, without you all is lost.
Earth cries out to you,
Come, come and help us.
To extend everywhere your wonderful realm
Come, come to us as God,
otherwise everything will perish.

## Chapter 3

### The Wondrous Power of Wisdom's Works in the Creation of the World and of Humankind

31. AFTER a whole eternity in the loving depths of God, Wisdom's power first burst forth in splendor outside the divine embrace when she made the light, the heavens, and the earth. St. John says: "*All things were made by the Word*" (Jn 1:3) *i.e.*, by Divine Wisdom. Solomon says, "*She is the mother and the designer of everything*" (Ws 7:2, 21). Notice that he does not just call her the craftswoman of the universe, but the mother, because the expert in a craft does not love and care for her work in the same way as a mother nurtures her child.

32. Having then created everything, Eternal Wisdom continues to abide in all things. She continues to "contain all, to sustain all, and to renew all" (Ws 1:7; 7:27). She, who is the essence of beauty and perfection, has fixed within her creation the magnificent order that we find there. She divided and she composed; she weighed and she measured; she took note of each thing individually. She spread out the heavens; she placed the sun, the moon, the stars and the planets in their proper paths; she laid the foundations of the earth; she set boundaries and laws for the sea and its deeps; she gave form to the mountains; she thought deeply and balanced it

all even to the very source-springs of the water. As she says herself, "*I was with God, ordering all things, with a precision so perfect, and a variety so pleasing, that it was like a game that I was playing for my own entertainment and that of my Father*" (Pr 8:30-31).

**33.** So wondrous is Wisdom's play that it cannot be expressed in human speech. It is most amazingly expressed in the marvelous variety of creatures that she brought forth into this universe. Before even considering the species of angels without number, or the grandeur of the stars, or the infinite variations in human personality, we can begin by admiring the changing moods of the seasons and of the weather, the wide variety of animals and their instincts, the multitudes of plant species, the matchless beauty of each kind of flower, the unique taste of each kind of fruit. "*Who is the one to whom Wisdom has communicated Herself?* (Hos 14:10). Only that person will understand the mysteries of nature.

**34.** Wisdom has revealed these mysteries to the saints, as we can see from their lives. There were times when they were so astounded to see the beauty, the harmony, and the order that Divine Wisdom poured out on even the smallest thing—like a bee, an ant, a grain of wheat, or an earthworm—that they were instantly filled with delight at the mere sight of it.

**35.** If the power and the sweetness of Wisdom shine forth so brilliantly in the beauty and order of the universe, how much more evident are these qualities in the creation of humankind! For the human being indeed is Wisdom's supreme creation, the living image[1] of her beauty and perfection, the most excellent container of her grace and of her treasures—her unique representative on earth. "*In your Wisdom you have so designed human beings that they are able to rule the creatures that you have made*" (Ws 9:2).

**36.** I wish I could honor properly Wisdom's glory as well as the beauty and power of her handiwork. I wish I could describe suitably the original beauty and excellence of the first human who received gifts fresh from her hand. But unfortunately, the awful sin that he committed and its terrible results which reach even as far as me—poor child of Eve that I am—have so dulled my understanding that I remain very limited in what I can say.

**37.** Figuratively speaking, we could say that in the human being, Wisdom created a likeness

1 Montfort uses here the word *image* and in no. 37 the word *portrait* both of which refer to Gen 1:26 where the Greek text uses the word *icon*.

and a brilliant expression of her own understanding, memory, and will. She implanted these three powers in the soul of man so that he could be the living portrait of divinity. In his heart she kindled a fire of pure love of God. She created his body shining and full of light. In the most compact way possible she incorporated in him all the different qualities of angels, of animals, and of all other creatures.

38. In the original human, everything was radiant without shadow, beautiful without defect, and pure without stain. All was harmonious without trace of discord, strain, or the slightest imperfection. The light of Wisdom illumined his mind so that he knew perfectly the Creator and all creatures. The grace of God completely filled his soul, so that he stood innocent and pleasing before the Most High. In his body, he was gifted with immortality. In his heart, which was free from any fear of death, he had a chaste love by which he loved God constantly, purely, and unconditionally for God's own sake. So divinely created was he that he lived in God in a continuous state of boundless joy, having no passion to overcome and no enemy to defend himself against. O the generosity of Divine Wisdom toward man! How happy he was in his original state! It is humanity's greatest misfortune to have lost Wisdom.

**39.** How great then is humanity's misfortune! The divine vessel is broken into a thousand pieces; the beautiful star falls from its heights; the sun is covered with the mud of earth. Man sins and loses his innocence, his beauty, and his immortality. Indeed, having lost all the blessings he has received, he becomes subject to countless ills. His spirit becomes dull and confused so that he no longer has understanding; his heart freezes so that he no longer loves God; his soul, now tarnished by sin, appears almost demon-like; with his passions fallen into disorder he can no longer control himself. For company he now has the evil spirits who seek him out and make him their slave. Even the other creatures have become enemies who attack him. In one brief moment man becomes the slave of demons, the object of God's anger, and the target of the powers of destruction. In his own eyes he appears so deep in shame that he goes off to hide himself. Cursed and condemned to death, he has been thrown out of the earthly paradise, and has lost his home in the heavens. He is destined to lead a desperate life on the resistant earth without hope of ever regaining happiness.[2] He will die like a criminal, and after death, along with all his descendants; he will be condemned body and soul to the fate of the fallen souls in hell. Such is the frightful

2 Cf. Gen 3:17-19, 24

condition into which humanity fell. Such is the fate pronounced on humankind by the justice of God.[3]

**40.** In this state Adam is quite desperate, without hope of receiving any help from the angels or from any other creatures. Nothing can repair his condition since by his sin all that in him that had been so beautifully designed and created has now become twisted and covered in filth. Barred from paradise and from the presence of God, he and his descendants remain under the firm judgment of God's justice. The gate of heaven has been closed, and there is no one to open it. The gate of hell has been opened, and there is no one to close it.

3 In this paragraph and the one that follows, Montfort paints a grim picture of the human condition after the fall of Adam and Eve. But he was already ecstatic, in the previous paragraph, about the previous state, bright and blissful, of the man living in paradise. We recognize the popular preacher who shakes his audience and then brings out more, as the apostle Paul had already done in his Letter to the Romans, the overabundance of grace, where sin abounded (Rom 5:15). Paragraphs 42-47 will show how this overabundance will be the effect of "an incomprehensible love that goes to excess;" love which is none other than that of Christ, Incarnate Wisdom.

## On Solitude

(Canticle 157:10-18)

**On the plains everything thrives**
**without any laborers' work.**
**By the hand of God this land**
**is virgin and fertile.**

**In the lovely groves, no sound of squabbles**
**among neighbors.**
**No chatting among the worldly,**
**no battles or shipwrecks.**

**The groves ring with sweet harmony of the**
**birds and the echoes,**
**The cries of animals, not those of ungodly men.**

**The eloquent silence of rocks and forests**
**Only preach peace, breathe only innocence.**

**Notice the town's madness?**
**Or those floods of iniquity,**
**Those frivolous melodies? No, not here, all is**
**fresh and calm.**

**The countryside holds none of those dangers.**
**The woods and the rocks are**
**the holy wise masters.**

**The rocks preach fidelity,**
**the weeds fruitfulness,**

**The streams purity, all things**
**love and obedience.**

**You can see flying overhead,**
**birds in their season.**
**At your feet all sorts of fish, and alongside all**
**kinds of animals.**

**The Creator's mighty hand which**
**formed this universe**
**Shines in these remote sites of innocent nature.**

## Chapter 4

### Wisdom's Astounding Kindness and Mercy toward Humankind before Her Incarnation

41. ETERNAL Wisdom is deeply touched by the misfortune of Adam and of all his descendants. It is with the greatest dismay that she sees her vessel of honor broken, her divine portrait made ugly, her masterpiece destroyed, and her closest image on earth overthrown. Tenderly she listens to man's broken-hearted cries. With pity she looks upon the sweat of his brow, the tears in his eyes, the straining of his shoulders, the sorrows and affliction of his heart and soul.

42. In my mind's eye I can almost see this lovable Queen convoking for a second time, as it were, a Council of the Blessed Trinity. During the Trinity's earlier meeting, the dialogue had, of course, centered upon the creation of humankind. This time it will consider the possibility of restoring humanity to its former communion with God.[1] It seems to me that in this new great council meeting there takes place a sort of contest between Eternal Wisdom and God's Justice.

43. I can almost hear Wisdom making the point that, even though human beings by reason

1 Montfort, inspired by Gen 1: 26, "Let us make man in our Image."...as Christian interpretations throughout the centuries, sees in the use of the plural, the expression of a Trinity project.

of their sin deserve the just condemnation which they share with the fallen angels, still it is right also to be merciful to them, for they have sinned not so much out of bad will, as through ignorance and weakness. On the one hand, she insists, it would be a great pity if this masterpiece of her creation were to be subject forever to the hostile powers, and that millions of descendants should be lost forever because of the sin of a single human ancestor.[2] On the other hand, she points out the places in heaven left vacant by the rebel angels, hinting that the time may be at hand to fill them again. She finishes by suggesting the great glory that would be given to God in time and in eternity if humankind could be saved.

**44.** I feel that I can hear the response of the voice of Justice arguing in turn that the decree of condemnation has already been pronounced against the whole race of humankind. Now it only remains for this decree to be executed to the full and without mercy just as it was for Lucifer and his followers. After all, man has shown his ingratitude for all the blessings so generously given him. In his pride and his refusal to obey God he has already followed Satan, and so in the same manner should he follow the fallen ones in the consequences of his

2 Certain passages of the Bible (Gen 6:1-4; 2Pet 2: 4; Jude 6) and the Jewish apocrypha (1 Henok) refer to the angels which were damned for having sinned against the established order of God.

actions, because Justice requires that sin should be punished.

45. Seeing clearly that there is no power in the universe able to make up for the sin of Adam or soften the justice and the anger of God, yet still wishing to save humans, whom she herself simply loves, Wisdom finds her own amazing way out of the deadlock. Unbelievably, out of the limitless generosity of her love, She offers this unimaginable solution: She herself will become the sacred offering required to make peace with the Father, to satisfy his justice, to calm his anger, to rescue us from slavery to the demonic powers and the fires of hell, and to win for us an eternity of blessed joy.

46. Her offer is accepted. The decision is taken: Eternal Wisdom—as Son of God—will become human in the time and in the circumstances appointed for it. About four thousand years will go by from the world's creation and the sin of Adam to the time of Wisdom's Incarnation. During this period Adam and his descendants will die as required by the divine judgment that is still in force, but in view of the coming Incarnation of the Son of God, they will receive the grace they need to obey the commandments and to do penance for their sins. Those who die in God's grace will descend into limbo to await their Savior who in the hour of liberation will open for them the gates of heaven.

**47.** During this whole period before the Incarnation, Eternal Wisdom demonstrated to humans in a thousand ways the friendship she had towards them, and the great desire she had to communicate her favors and to be in contact with them. "*My delight is to be with the children of humanity*" (Pr 8:31). "*She turned in every direction to seek those worthy of her*" (Ws 6:17) that is, persons worthy of her friendship, worthy of her treasures, worthy of her own self. "*She wandered among different peoples; passing into holy souls, she makes them friends of God and prophets*" (Ws 7:27). It is she alone who formed all the holy patriarchs, the friends of God, the prophets and the saints of the Old and New Testament. It was Wisdom who inspired the saints, who spoke by the mouth of the prophets, and directed them in their ways, gave them light to resolve their doubts, held them up in their weaknesses, and delivered them from every evil.

**48.** The Holy Spirit has told the stories of the ancients in the tenth chapter of the Book of Wisdom in His own words:[3]

[1a] *It was Wisdom who protected the first man ever made, the father of the world, who had been created all alone—Adam.* [1b] *It was she*

3 In his rereading of the beginning of history until the exodus, the author of Wisdom does not mention any proper names and rather dwells on the typical actions of the characters. For the benefit of his readers, Montfort nevertheless takes the liberty of identifying them. In our modern Bibles, this identification is made in notes and commentaries.

*who rescued him from his fall,* [2] *and gave him the strength to rule over all things.*[3] *When in his wrath a wicked man—Cain—deserted her, that man destroyed himself by murdering his brother.*[4] *When because of him the earth was drowned, it was Wisdom again who saved it. She piloted the upright man—Noah—on ordinary wooden boards.*

[5] *And when, by acting together in wickedness, the nations had been thrown into confusion, she singled out the upright man—Abraham—preserved him blameless before God, and fortified him against pity for his child, Isaac.* [6] *She it was who, while the godless were dying, saved the upright man—Lot—as he fled from the fire raining down on the Five Cities.* [7] *In witness against their evil ways a barren land still smokes, where plants bear fruit that never ripens, and where, as a monument to the unbelieving soul, there stands a pillar of salt.* [8] *For, by ignoring the path of Wisdom, not only did they suffer the loss of knowing the good, but they left the world a memorial to their foolishness, so that their crimes could not pass unnoticed.*

**49.** [9] *But Wisdom delivered her servants from their ordeals.* [10] *The upright man—Jacob—fleeing from the anger of his brother—Esau—was led by her along straight paths. She showed him the kingdom of God and taught him the* *knowledge of holy things. She brought him success in his labors and gave him full return for all his efforts. 11 She stood by him against grasping and oppressive men, and she made him rich. 12 She protected him from his enemies and saved him from the traps they set for him. In an arduous struggle she awarded him the prize to teach him that piety (wisdom) is stronger than all.*

*13 She did not forsake the upright man—Joseph—when he was sold, but snatched him away from sin; she accompanied him down into the pit, 14 Nor did she abandon him in his chains until she had brought him the sceptre of a kingdom and authority over his unjust masters, thus exposing as liars those who had betrayed him, and giving him honor everlasting.*

*15 It was Wisdom who delivered a holy people—the Hebrews—an innocent race, from a nation of oppressors. 16 She entered the soul of the servant of the Lord—Moses—and withstood fearsome kings with wonders and signs. 17 To the holy people she gave the wages of their labors; she guided them by a marvelous road; she was herself their shelter by day and their starlight through the night. 18 She brought them across the Red Sea, leading them through an immensity of water, but she drowned their enemies, and then spat them out from the depths of the abyss. 20a So the upright despoiled the godless. 20b Lord, they glorified your holy name, and with one accord praised your protecting hand; 21 for Wisdom opened the mouths of the dumb*[4] *and gave speech to the tongues of babes.*[5]

**50.** In the next chapter of the Book of Wisdom, the Holy Spirit describes the various troubles from which Eternal Wisdom rescued Moses and the Israelites while they were in the desert. To these we may add all those who were delivered from great dangers, whether in the Old or the New Testament. For example, there was Daniel who was delivered from the lions' den; Susannah who was saved from false accusations of a crime; the three young men saved from the furnace in Babylon; St. Peter from his prison; St. John from the cauldron of boiling oil; and countless martyrs and confessors who were delivered from the torments inflicted on them physically and the lies that ruined their reputations. All these were delivered and healed by Eternal Wisdom: "O Lord, those who pleased you from the beginning were healed by Wisdom" (Ws 9:18).

**51.** And now let us exclaim: "A thousand times blessed is the soul in whom Wisdom has made her dwelling! Whatever battles they have to fight, they will be victorious; whatever dangers threaten them, they will escape; whatever

4 Cf. Mk 7:37

5 Cf. Is 35:6 and Ps 8:2-3

sorrows overwhelm them, they will find comfort and consolation. Whatever humiliations they have to endure, they will be lifted up and glorified in time and in eternity."

## Praises of God for His Blessings

(Canticle 52:1-2; 51:3, 9, 13; 52:6, 9, 11)

Let us forever bless the Lord for His great gifts.
Bless Him holy Angels, praise His majesty.
To His kindness render unending,
lasting praise.
Let us forever bless the Lord for His great gifts.

O how good a Father, He takes great care of us.
He supports us one and all even in our misery
Let us forever…

His gentle Providence orders all things firmly,
Leads everything wisely, without
anyone being aware.
Let us forever …

Showing no prejudice He seeks only to forgive,
His great joy is to give, He is happy
when He does so.
Let us forever…

He searches the dust for the innocent poor
To exalt them on high, resplendent with light.
Let us forever …

He has taken for His temple both my
body and my heart,
It is there that His great splendor shines
brightly night and day.
Let us forever…

His kindness upholds me, His light instructs me
His beauty ravishes me, His love enraptures me.
Let us forever…

God alone is my tenderness, God alone
is my support.
God alone is all I have, my life and my wealth.
Let us forever bless the Lord for His great gifts.

# Chapter 5

## Eternal Wisdom's Amazing Excellence

52. SINCE the Holy Spirit has taken such care to show us Wisdom's excellence in the Eighth Chapter of the Book of Wisdom, it will be enough for us just to recall these words of Scripture, to which I shall add a very short commentary.[1]

53. *[1] How powerfully she reaches from one end of the world to the other, and how gently she rules the whole world for its own benefit.*

Nothing is gentler than Wisdom. She is sweetness itself by nature; in her there is no bitterness; she is kind to those who love her, and in her company there is no anxiety. She is gentle in her approach, and she does no violence to anyone. So quiet and gentle is she that one would scarcely recognize her presence in the accidents and upsets that happen in life: but since her power cannot be overcome, she moves all things surely, yet invisibly, toward their true purpose, according to her secret ways that very often escape the observation of human beings.

1 This is the only time that Montfort comments on a biblical text verse by verse or by small groups of verses. It is always Scripture that inspires him and that is the only focus of his personal meditation according to the tradition known as *lectio divina*. It also allows him to explain to his readers his concern for bringing it up to date.

Following her example, the disciple of Wisdom aspires to be: "gently powerful and powerfully gentle."

**54.** [2] ***Wisdom I loved and sought from my youth; I resolved to have her as my bride.***

Whoever wants to acquire the great treasure, which is Wisdom, had better follow the example of Solomon in seeking her: (1) *early*, if possible, even from a very tender age (2) *spiritually* and purely, as a chaste bridegroom pursuing his bride (3) *perseveringly*, until the end, until one really has obtained her. It is certain that Eternal Wisdom loves souls so much that she will go so far as to espouse them, to enter into a spiritual yet true marriage with them, a union which the world does not know, yet one which we find examples of in history.

**55.** [3] ***The glory of Wisdom's noble birth is made even brighter by her intimate sharing of God's life, for the master of all has always loved her.***

Wisdom is truly God. That is the glory of her noble origin. God the Father proclaims the delight he takes in her. [2]That is the measure of how she is loved.

**56.** [4] ***Indeed she shares the secrets of God's knowledge, and she directs his works.***

2 Cf. Mt 3:17

Wisdom alone is the one who "*enlightens every person coming into this world*;" (Jn 1:9). She alone has come down from heaven to teach us the secrets of God. Indeed, we have no other true Master[3] than Wisdom Incarnate, who is Jesus Christ. Thus, it is that she orders all the works of God and particularly of the saints. She does this by guiding them to know what they must do, and by giving them a taste and an experience of what she wants to communicate to them.

57. [5] *If, in this life, one longs for wealth, what is a greater treasure than Wisdom whose work is everywhere?* [6] *Or if the human intellect achieves something, who has played a greater part in it than Wisdom, who is the designer of all?*[4] [7] *Or if it be holiness you love, know that virtues are also the fruit of her labors, since it is she who teaches temperance and prudence, justice and fortitude; nothing in life is more useful for human beings.*

Solomon makes us see that it is only Wisdom whom we should love; for it is from her that we can expect to receive all we need—whether it be material means, knowledge of nature's hidden ways, spiritual gifts, or the theological and the cardinal virtues.

3 Cf. Mt 23: 8,10

4 Cf. Jn 1:3

**58.** [8] *Or if you are eager to sound the depths of understanding, she knows the past and she forecasts the future. She knows how to formulate proverbs and solve riddles; she has foreknowledge of signs, wonders, and the unfolding of the ages and the times.*

Whoever wants to have a really extraordinary knowledge of the workings of grace and of nature, a knowledge holy and deep, that goes beyond the abstract and the superficial—such a one should make every effort to acquire Wisdom. For, without her, no one is of any account before God;[5] no matter how learned he might appear.

**59.** [9] *I therefore determined to take her to share my life, knowing that she would be my counselor in prosperity and that she would comfort me in cares and sorrow.*

Which of us could consider themselves poor if they have Wisdom who is so generous? Which of us could imagine themselves sad if they are with Wisdom who is so sweet, so tender, so beautiful? Yet, among those who seek Wisdom which of them can truly say along with Solomon, "*I am determined*?" As far as sincere resolution is concerned, most people have not gone to the furthest limits; they are content with mere dreams and weak decisions. Or at best,

5 Ws 3:17

their so-called 'resolution' wanders weakly first to one side and then to the other and finally grows indifferent. That is why they fail to find Wisdom.

**60.** [10] *Thanks to her I shall be admired by the masses and honored, even though I am young, by the elders.* [11] *I shall be considered as shrewd as a judge, and the great will be amazed at me.* [12] *They will wait on my silences, and pay attention when I speak; if I speak at some length, they will place their hands over their lips.* [13] *By means of her, immortality will be mine, I shall leave an everlasting memory to my successors.* [14] *I shall govern peoples, and nations will be subject to me.*

Regarding these self-congratulating words of the wise king, St. Gregory makes the following reflection: "Those who were chosen by God to be authors of the scriptures were so filled with the Spirit that they were carried, we should say, out of themselves. They were so merged with the divine Being who held them that it was as though they became the very 'tongue' of God, so that they considered only God in everything they said. They spoke of themselves as if they were speaking of someone else."

**61.** [15] *At the sound of my name, even the most terrifying kings will be afraid; I shall show myself kind to my people and brave in battle.*

*[16] When I return home I shall take my ease with her, for nothing is bitter in her company; when life is shared with her there is no pain, nothing but pleasure and joy. [17] Having meditated on all this, I have come to the conclusion that immortality comes from one's relationship with Wisdom, [18] noble contentment accompanies her friendship, inexhaustible riches are found in her activities, understanding dwells in close companionship with her and fame in conversing with her and so I have traveled every possible path, seeking how to make her mine.*

Having summarized all that he had said, the wise king, Solomon, concluded: "*I turned in every direction to seek her.*" To acquire Wisdom one has to seek her passionately, that is to say, one must be ready to leave everything,[6] suffer everything, and undertake everything to possess her. There are few who find her, because there are so few who seek her in a manner that is worthy of her.

**62.** In the Seventh Chapter of the Book of Wisdom, the Holy Spirit speaks again of her Excellence.

*[22] For within her is a spirit: intelligent, holy, the only one of her kind, showing herself in many forms, hard to grasp, flowing in movement, cutting to the very heart of things, without stain,*

6 Cf. Mk 10:28-30

*full of light, not subject to harm, wishing good to every person, clever, irresistible, always doing good,* [23] *friendly to human beings, steadfast, dependable, untroubled, almighty, all-seeing, penetrating, all-intelligent, pure, and most delicate in all her ways.* [24] *For Wisdom is quicker to move than any motion; she is so pure that she enters all things and fills them completely.* [25] *She is a breath of the power of God, a pure outpouring of the glory of the Almighty; so nothing impure can find its way into her.*

Finally, *she is to human beings an inexhaustible treasure, and those who acquire it win God's friendship, commended to him by her gifts of instruction* (Ws 7:14).

**63.** After such powerful and tender praises spoken by the Spirit to show us the beauty, the excellence, and the treasures of Wisdom, is there anyone who would not pursue her with all possible effort? This is all the more true because Wisdom is an infinite treasure destined for all of us; she is the goal for which all humans have been created. Finally, she herself has an infinite desire to give herself to us.

## Desires of Incarnate Wisdom

(Canticle 103:4-7, 1)

Jesus uncreated Wisdom, come to me.
Jesus incarnate Wisdom, come to me.
What is sweeter than to be with you?
But what hell to be without you!

O Wisdom, God made man, come to me.
I acknowledge you, I call you, come to me.
With you and your cross
I shall be happier than any king.

O my powerful princess, come to me.
O my charming mistress, come to me.
To be with you bestows more pleasure
Than our heart could ever imagine.

O my immortal spouse, come to me.
My beautiful one, my faithful one, come to me.
With you I am stronger
Than hell or death.

Forgive, Divine Wisdom, my ardor
For you are the mistress of my heart.
Hasten to my assistance,
Give ear to my pleas.

# Chapter 6

## Wisdom's Urgent Desire to Give Herself to Humankind

64. THERE is a bond of intimacy between humankind and Wisdom that is so deep that it is absolutely beyond human understanding: Wisdom exists for each one of us; and each one of us exists for Wisdom. *"Wisdom is an infinite treasure for humankind"* (Ws 7:14) in ways that are not so evident for angels or other creatures. This friendship of Wisdom for humanity is based on the fact that by their very creation humans sum up in themselves all her marvelous qualities. A human being reflects the 'big world' or universal dimension of Wisdom by being her living image; at the same time every human person is, in a sense, a 'little world' of Wisdom, her representative here on earth. Out of her great love for humanity, she took on our human nature by becoming incarnate and she even delivered herself up to death for the salvation of mere human beings. Thus she shows how deeply she loves each human being as her brother or sister, as her friend, her disciple, her pupil, the gift won by her blood sacrifice, and the co-heir of her kingdom. So true is this that whenever one refuses her love or snatches from her the heart of any human being, she feels it as an immeasurable violence done to herself.

**65.** This supremely beautiful and attractive personage desires our human friendship so ardently that she deliberately wrote a book to attract us. In this work she unveils for us not only her qualities but also her heartfelt desire for us. Her book is like a love letter designed to win the affection of the beloved of her soul. So urgent are Wisdom's desires for the hearts of humans, so tender are her advances, so loving are her appeals and promises, that to hear Wisdom speak you would not think she was the queen of heaven and earth, but rather you might imagine that she needed humans in order to be happy herself. That, however, is not the case.

**66.** At times she seeks humans on the highways and byways; at other times she climbs the mountain peaks; sometimes she comes to the city gates; or else she enters the marketplaces or the courts, crying out as loudly as possible: "*O you humans, you children of humankind! It is you I have been calling to for so long! To you I lift my voice* (Pr 8:4); you are my desire; it is you I seek; it is you whom I claim for my own. Listen and come to me; I want to make you happy.[1] To attract them powerfully, she says: *15* "*Through me* and by my grace *do kings reign and princes command,* and rulers bear the staff and wear the crown. *16* I am the one who inspires lawmakers with the knowledge to make wise

1 Paraphrase of Pr 8:32

laws for the governance of states; I am the one who transmits power to magistrates so that they can administer justice fairly and without fear.

**67.** [17] *I love those who love me, and whoever searches eagerly for me will find me;* (Pr 8:17) and finding me, will find an abundance of all blessings; [18] for riches, glory, honors, public esteem, true pleasures, and authentic virtues are with me; [19] and it is incomparably better for a person to possess me than to possess all the gold and all the silver in the world, or all the precious jewels and the goods of the whole universe. [20] I guide those who come to me by the ways of justice and prudence, and I enrich them with an inheritance that belongs to my true children; I fulfil all their desires. [31] Be convinced that my sweetest pleasure "*and my dearest delight is to converse with and to dwell among the children of humankind.*"

**68.** "*So now, my children listen to me. Happy are they who keep my ways. Pay attention to my instruction; be wise and reject it not. Happy is the one who listens to me, who waits for me every day at the entrance to my house, who stands expectantly at my door. Whoever finds me will find life;* and will draw from my well the salvation and the goodness of the Lord. *But whoever sins* against me *will wound their own souls. All those who hate me love death*" (Pr 8:32-36).

**69.** After all that she has done most tenderly and most engagingly to attract the friendship of humans, she still fears that their fearful respect for her shining splendor and exalted majesty might hold them back from approaching her. This is why she lets them know her true message:

*"Access to her is easy. Those who love her see her easily. She goes ahead of those who desire her; She is the first to show herself to them. Whoever gets up early to seek her will have no trouble, but will find her sitting at the door, waiting"* (Ws 6:13-15).

**70.** Finally, in her desire to approach closer to humanity and to give humans a more visible evidence of her love, Eternal Wisdom took on our human nature, even going so far as to become a child and one of the poor. She even went to the extreme of dying on the cross for humankind. During his earthly life, how often did he Incarnate Wisdom cry out:

*"Come to me, come to me all of you!* (Mt 11:28). *It is I, fear not!"* (Mk 6:50; Mt 14:27; Jn 6:30). Why do you fear? I am one of you; I love you. Do you fear because you are sinners? Ah! But then you are just the ones I seek; *I am the friend of sinners* (Mt 11:19). Is it because you wilfully strayed away from the fold? Ah! But then, *"I am the Good Shepherd"* (Jn 10:11). Is it because you are

burdened with sins, covered all over with filth, overcome with sorrows? Ah! But that is why you should come to me; for I will unburden you, and I will comfort you.[2]

**71.** Desiring on the one hand to show her love by dying in our place so as to save us, and unwilling on the other hand, to leave us behind, she found a wonderful and secret way to die and to live at the same time, and to remain with humanity until the end of time. This is her wonderfully creative gift of the Eucharist. To fulfil her love's wish, Eternal Wisdom did not hesitate to turn the whole of the natural order upside down! If she didn't choose to hide herself in a diamond or other precious jewel, it was because she did not want to remain outside of us, however near she might be to us. No, she chose to hide herself under the appearance of a small piece of bread—the basic food of humans—so that she could be eaten and in that way enter into the depths of the human heart and take her delight there.[3] One saint has prayed: "O God, most generously pouring himself out because of his desire for humankind."[4]

**72.** If we fail to be moved by the urgency of Wisdom, by her loving pursuits, and by the demonstrations of her friendship, how shall we

2 Cf. Mt 11:28-29

3 St. John Chrysostom

4 Blessed Guerric of Igny

face up to our ingratitude and our hardness of heart? If instead of listening to her we close our ears; if, instead of seeking her, we fly from her; if, instead of honoring her and loving her, we reject her and offend her, what is the measure of our cruelty! And what will be the punishment that will come upon us even in this life! *For, by ignoring the path of Wisdom, not only did they suffer the loss of knowing what is good, but they left the world a memorial to their foolishness, so that their offenses could not pass unnoticed* (Ws 10:8). Three misfortunes in life fall upon those who do not take the trouble to acquire Wisdom. They fall into: (1) ignorance and blindness; (2) foolish mistakes; (3) sin and scandal. But a greater misfortune awaits them at death, when they hear what they did not expect to hear: the reproaches of Wisdom:

"*I called and you did not answer me*" (Pr 1:24). I held out my hands to you all day long, and you rejected me; I waited for you, seated at your door, and you did not come to me. "*Therefore, for my part, I shall laugh at your distress*" (Pr 1:26). I no longer have ears to hear your cries, eyes to see your tears, a heart to be moved by your weeping, or hands to reach out to you!"

And what then will be their distress in hell! Read the words that the Holy Spirit spoke about these unfortunate ones—about the moans, the regrets, the despair of the hardened souls in hell, who recognized their foolishness too late and suffered their misfortune for having despised the Wisdom of God. They begin to speak wisely, but in hell.[5]

**73.** Let us then desire Wisdom and seek single-mindedly for her. And another scripture says: "*There is nothing more desirable than Wisdom*" (Pr 3:15). Whatever gifts of God you have, whatever heavenly treasures you desire, if you do not desire Wisdom, you desire something less than her. If we only knew what this infinite treasure of Wisdom destined for us humans really is, and I confess that I have said less than nothing about her! We would sigh day and night after her. We would fly to the ends of the earth; we would gladly pass through fire and sword, if necessary, to win her. But we must beware of making a mistake in our choice of Wisdom for there are several kinds to choose from.

5 Cf. Ws 5:14

## Devotion to the Sacred Heart

(Canticle 44:2-3, 9, 12, 14-15)

Love this heart for it loves us,
Love is repaid with love.
Love with overflowing love
Purely night and day.

All heaven kneels before this heart,
Calling earth to adore it.
Let us in justice then adore,
For it is the heart of God.

Let us go to melt our coldness
In this Heart the burning bush.
Let us there all graces draw
From His heart's abundant store.

In our troubles and afflictions,
In our most painful trials,
In this heart, let's place our hope;
It is our heart; it is ours.

This heart is our life's model,
Let us all assume its mind;
Heart to heart, we follow it
In all its ways and actions.

In famine and abundance,
In joy as well as sorrow,
In what we do and what we think,
We stay one with it always.

## Chapter 7

### Choosing True Wisdom

**74.** GOD has his Wisdom; this is the unique and genuine Wisdom that is to be desired and pursued as a great treasure. But the corrupted spirit of the 'world' also has its wisdom; and it is to be regarded with distaste and even rejected as something harmful and spoiled. The philosophers also have their wisdom; this too we should not accept, for it is of little use, and it is often dangerous to the health of our souls. Up to now we have spoken of the Wisdom of God to souls who are mature,[1] as St. Paul says, but lest our readers be deceived by the false brilliance of the world's wisdom, we undertake now to unmask for them the hidden but terribly dangerous nature of its misleading appeal.

**75.** Worldly wisdom is that of which it is said: "I will destroy the wisdom of the wise" (1 Co1:19). The wisdom of the flesh is the enemy of God. "*Such wisdom does not come from on high; but is a wisdom that is worldly, lustful, and devilish*" (Jm 3:15). This wisdom of the world supports the following values: conforming totally to the fashions and slogans of 'society'; striving relentlessly for status and fame; executing our disguised but fierce strategies to secure

1 1 Cor 2:6

pleasure and material advancement. Of course, all this is done—not in an ugly and open manner by committing some obvious crime. No, it is done in an underhanded and clever way that is meant to deceive. If it were done openly and in an exaggerated way, it would simply be called 'bizarre behavior' and not regarded as an example of 'wisdom.'

**76.** Society judges a person to be wise if he is a smart businessman—one who can always turn a deal to advantage without appearing to do so. Such a person has mastered the art of deceiving simple trusting people without their even noticing it. This one says one thing, but is thinking another. He is always ready to adapt appearance and way of speech to flatter and win over anyone he wants to exploit for purposes of his own. But for the honor of God or the interests of God this person has little concern. He is skilled at inventing unholy alliances between truth and falsehood, between the gospel and the world, between virtue and sin, between Jesus Christ and Beelzebub. Such a one tries to appear like a 'good fellow,' but never like a holy person. He mocks, twists the meaning of, or condemns outright any practice of piety that is not to his liking. In short, a wise person of the world is one who conducts himself solely on the basis of his fleshly desires and human tendency to think up clever reasons to justify everything he does. Although he would occasionally like to appear as if he were a 'good Christian,' he would never put himself to the trouble of trying to please God or to do penance for the sins committed against the Divine Majesty.

77. The seven motivations of the worldly man or woman are built on the following values: upholding his 'public image', guarding her reputation, following all the latest fashions, enjoying himself, pursuing her advancement and success, maintaining a proper outward image of himself; and being considered a friendly and entertaining companion. These are the seven foundations—quite innocent to his mind—on which the worldly person tries to build what he or she thinks of as the 'good life.' The so-called 'virtues' that these worldly people hold in esteem are: projecting an image of great bravery, cultivating a polished politeness, being clever in politics, cheating other people without seeming to do so, maintaining an outward show of courage, mastering a 'smooth manner' of doing things, developing a style that will win favor from those in power. The 'serious sins' according to these standards are: loudness and rudeness, a clumsy lack of politeness, self-consciousness, a narrow-minded outlook.

78. The person of the world follows the commandments of the world as faithfully as possible:

1. You shall know your way around in high society.
2. You shall keep up the appearance of one who knows his way about.
3. You shall be on top of your career and manage its advancement.
4. You shall hang on with all your might to what is yours.
5. You shall always climb the ladder to higher success.
6. You shall make friends who will be useful to your career.
7. You shall associate mostly with people in high places.
8. You shall always have a good time.
9. You shall never get depressed.
10. You shall avoid looking 'different' from the fashion-leaders, or being easily tricked by the clever, or appearing narrow-minded in your views.

**79.** Never has the world been as corrupt as it is now, because never has it been so clever in evil ways, so wise in its own opinions, so able to use people for its own political ends. It uses the truth to dress up its lies, the language of virtue to justify its sins, and even the maxims of Jesus Christ to lend authority to its own worldly standards. And it does all this so cleverly that even the wise ones of God are often deceived. "*The number of those who are fools* according to the world *or wise ones* according to the world *is infinite*" (Qo 1:15).

**80.** The wisdom of the world that St. James speaks about is the excessive desire for the things of this earth. This is the hidden 'credo' that worldly people believe in when they are attached to their possessions. For such people their whole effort in life is to get rich; they think up lawsuits and invent court cases with the sole aim of acquiring new property or holding on to old property. Most of the time they neither think, nor speak, nor act from any other motive than their own material advancement. At the same time they give almost no thought and only superficial obedience 'for the sake of appearance,' to matters that concern their eternal salvation—like prayer, Holy Communion, and confession.

**81.** Carnal wisdom is the desire for pleasure. It is the hidden 'credo' of the 'worldly-wise' whose lives are spent pursuing sensual gratification even though they do it secretly. It includes those who: are always looking forward to a party; avoid anything which might inconvenience or discipline their body, such as fasts, or austerities; for the most part think only of drinking, eating, playing games, making jokes, and entertaining themselves with empty pastimes; and are always in search of a comfortable bed, an interesting game, a delicious banquet, and the company of stylish people. After they have managed to indulge themselves to the limit without any pangs of conscience, and without falling out of favor or damaging their health, then these people seek out 'the least scrupulous' confessor that they can find. By 'least scrupulous' they mean those easy-going confessors who don't do their duty. In this way, at a cheap price they can have a plenary indulgence and stay comfortable in their undisciplined and wishy-washy lifestyle. I say 'at a cheap price' because those who are wise according to the flesh usually say only a few prayers or give stingy alms to the poor for their penance; they avoid anything that might inflict some hardship on their bodies.

**82. Diabolical wisdom** is the desire for the honors and esteem of the world. This is the hidden '*credo*' of those wise ones of the world who aspire—though secretly—to titles, honors, status, and high-ranking positions. Their aim is to be seen, promoted, talked about and applauded by others; they have no other motive behind their studies, their hard work, their struggles, and all their words and actions, than the esteem and the praise of worldly people. They want to pass for devout persons, or scholars, or military leaders, or eminent lawyers, or in general for men of merit and distinction worthy of everyone's consideration. They cannot stand to be overlooked or blamed for anything, and they hide their faults and reveal in public only what they think looks good.

**83.** With Jesus Christ our Lord, we ought to detest and condemn these three kinds of false wisdom, so that we can acquire true wisdom—which does not seek: to promote personal ambition, to dwell in an earthly abode nor in the hearts of those who seek an easy life, to follow whatever is grand and elevated in the eyes of this world. In fact, true wisdom holds these things to be hateful.

**84.** Besides this worldly wisdom, which is dangerous and deserving of condemnation, there is the natural wisdom of the philosophers: this is the wisdom pursued so fervently by the Egyptians and the Greeks. The Greeks seek their wisdom. Those who had acquired something of this wisdom were called sages or magi by the ancients. "*The Gentiles look for wisdom*" (1Cor 1:22). What they found was a higher insight into the fundamental principles of nature. This is the science of which Adam in his innocent state had full knowledge, this is the wisdom that was also given abundantly to Solomon, and in the course of time, to certain other renowned people, as we know from history.

**85.** The philosophers of our time promote their own argumentation as though it were a way to acquire this wisdom. The alchemists too boast of their secret formulas[2] for finding the 'philosopher's stone,' in which they imagine wisdom to be hidden. Admittedly, scholastic philosophy, seen from a Christian perspective, does indeed open the mind and expand its capacity for higher knowledge, but it cannot give access to this 'natural knowledge' so prized in ancient times.

**86.** Still more useless and dangerous is the science of 'chemistry' or 'alchemy' which focuses on dissolving material substances into their constituent elements. Even though it may have validity in its own right, alchemy has deceived many people in the goals that it proposes under the pretext of finding the philosopher's stone. I have personal experience of this, and I don't doubt the devil makes use of it in leading people to waste their money, their time, and maybe

2 The formulas is an esoteric tradition which claims the secret revelations that Moses had received on Mt. Sinai. A current Christian of the Cabal was developed under the influence of Pie de la Mirandole (+1494).

even the grace of their souls. No science makes grander promises, and no science is more simplistic in the means it advertises. The alchemists promise you health, healing, a long life, and all manner of miracles which the more simple-minded people take to be supernatural. They claim to accomplish their 'miracles' by means of the philosopher's stone, or by some magic powder that they sprinkle on a metallic object to change it into silver or gold. There are several people who claim to be experts in this science. They call themselves 'cabbalists,' and they keep their secrets so strictly that they would rather die than reveal them.

**87.** They appeal to the following authorities: (1) They claim to have found the secret of the philosopher's stone in a secret book of Solomon, *The Clavicle of Solomon*, but this is a false and wicked claim. (2) They quote the apocryphal Seventh Book of Esdras[3], in which it is written that God gave Esdras a heavenly liquid to drink, which imparted wisdom to him. (3) They quote Raymond Lully and several other philosophers who claim to have found this philosopher's stone. (4) Finally, to disguise

3 It is difficult to identify this 7th book of Esdras to which Montfort refers. Recent critical editions in French (*Écrits apocryphes Christians*, t. 1, Bibliothèque de la Pléiade, 1997) include several writings attributed to Esdras, including the 5th and 6th books of Esdras, but not the 7th. It must be said that the apocrypha often have alternative titles, which makes it difficult to locate the book mentioned by Montfort.

their deceptions under the cloak of piety, they say that it is a gift God gives to those who have long sought it, and who have merited it by their prayers and good works.

**88.** I share with you my experience of their fantasies and illusions about this false science, so that you may not be led astray like so many others; for I know quite a few people who were forced to admit they had been tricked only after wasting considerable time and money in the pursuit of this secret, having been deceived by the most plausible and pious of pretexts. I don't necessarily doubt that this philosopher's stone might exist. The scholar Delrio demonstrates its possibility, while others deny it. Whatever the case, it is not appropriate and may even be dangerous for a Christian to pursue it. To do so is to show a lack of appreciation for Jesus Christ, Incarnate Wisdom, in whom are "*all the treasures of the Wisdom and the Knowledge of God*" (Col 2:3); and it is to resist the Holy Spirit, who says: "*Do not try to understand things that are too difficult for you, or try to discover what is beyond your capacities*" (Si 3:22).

**89.** Let us live, then, in Jesus Christ—Eternal and Incarnate Wisdom—outside of whom there is only deceit and death, for he has said: "*I am the Way, the Truth, and the Life*" (Jn 14:6). In the next chapter we shall look at Wisdom's effects in souls.

## Chapter 8

### The Splendid Effects That Eternal Wisdom Produces in the Souls of Those Who Possess Her

**90.** THIS lovely Queen, whose nature it is to "*love the good*" (Ws 7:22), particularly the good of humankind, takes the greatest delight in communicating herself to humans. Thus, the Holy Spirit affirms that "*she goes about, seeking among all the peoples of the world, humans who are worthy of her, passing into holy souls making them into friends of God and prophets*" (Ws 7:27).

In ancient times she passed into the soul of God's servant Moses, and communicated to him the abundant light he needed to see great visions, and also the marvelous strength he needed to perform great deeds, and to accomplish his wondrous victories. "*She entered into the soul of a servant of the Lord and withstood fearsome kings with wonders and signs*" (Ws 10:16). When Divine Wisdom enters into a soul, she brings with her all sorts of blessings and shares untold treasures: "*In her company all good things came to me, and at her hands wealth beyond measure*" (Ws 7:11). To the truth of this Solomon gives witness, after having himself received Wisdom.

**91.** Here are some of the countless ways, often hidden and unnoticed, by which Wisdom communicates herself:

**92.** 1) She communicates her own spirit full of Light: "*I prayed, and understanding was given to me. I begged humbly in prayer, and the spirit of Wisdom came to me*" (Ws 7:7). Upon us humans, Wisdom's delicate and discerning spirit confers good judgment and a capacity for appropriate decisions very like that of Solomon himself. "*I shall be considered to be as clever as a judge, and those who are powerful will be amazed at me*" (Ws 8:11).

**93.** Wisdom confers upon humans the great 'science' of holiness, as well as knowledge of the natural sciences—even the most deeply secret ones—as these become useful to humanity.

*Or if you are eager for wide experience, she knows the past; she forecasts the future; she has foreknowledge of signs and wonders, and of the unfolding of the ages and the times* (Ws 8:8). *She conferred upon Jacob the 'science of the saints'* (Ws 10:10). *She taught him the knowledge of holy things.*

*Upon Solomon she conferred a true science of nature* (Ws 7:17). She revealed to him countless secrets that had never been known before. "*And now I understand everything, invisible or visible"* (Ws 7:21).

**94.** From this infinite source of light the great Doctors of the Church received their wonderful knowledge which so inspires us. St. Thomas Aquinas explicitly acknowledges this secret source. And we too can recognize that it is not a dry or barren kind of knowledge that is given, but indeed a knowledge filled with light and sweetness, a powerful and effective knowledge that touches the heart even as it illuminates the mind.

**95.** Wisdom gives humans not only the light to know truth, but also the capacity to share it with others. That which holds all things together *"knows every word that is said"* (Ws 1:7). Indeed, Wisdom has intimate knowledge of speech, and it is she who gives us a capacity to speak well. *"For Wisdom opened the mouth of the dumb and made eloquent the tongues of babes"* (Ws 10:21).

She untied Moses' tongue and delivered him of his speech defect. She inspired the prophets with words that have the power *"to uproot, to destroy, to disperse, to build, and to plant"* (Jer 1:10), even though they themselves felt they could speak no better than children.

It was Wisdom who gave the apostles the capacity to preach the gospel everywhere *"announcing the great deeds of God"* (Acts 2:11). "She made of their mouths an abundant outpouring of the word."[1]

Just as in eternity Wisdom is the Word, so has she spoken in this dimension of time, and so she continues to speak. Her word is the foundation and the renewal of all things. She has already spoken by the prophets and through the apostles. And she will speak until the end of time by the mouths of whomever she chooses.

**96.** 2) The words by which Divine Wisdom communicates are not ordinary human words: they are divine words. Not merely human words but God's word.[2] They are powerful, moving, and penetrating words. *"The word of God is alive and active: it cuts more finely than any two-edged sword"* (Hb 4:12). Wisdom's words spring from the heart of the one through whom she speaks, and they touch the hearts of those who listen. This is the gift that Solomon was referring to when he said that *"God had given him the grace to speak according to the feelings of his heart"* (Ws 7:15).

1 Part of the 3rd verse of the hymn of Vespers of Pentecost *Come Holy Spirit.*

2 Cf. 1 Th 2:13

**97.** These are the words of power that our Lord promised His apostles:

"*I will give you such eloquence and a strength and wisdom that your opponents will not be able to resist it*" (Lk 21:15). There are few such preachers today who have this gift of the word, and who can say with St. Paul: "*We speak the Wisdom of God*" (1 Cor 2:7). Most preachers speak according to their own natural lights, or draw upon what they have read in books, but not *according to what Divine Wisdom has inspired them* to feel (Ws 7:15) *from the abundance that Wisdom has communicated to their hearts* (Mt 12:34). This is why we see so few conversions brought about by the word. If a preacher had really received the gift of speech from Wisdom, his listeners would not be able to resist his words, as was the case in earlier times. Those who listened to St. Stephen "*could not resist the Wisdom and the Spirit who was speaking*" (Acts 6:10). Such a preacher would speak *with so much unction and authority* (Mk 1:22), that his word would not return to him empty.

**98.** 3) We know that Eternal Wisdom is not only the object of the Eternal Father's delight but she is also the joy of the angels. So to the one who possesses her, she is the beginning of the purest, the sweetest, and most exquisite of consolations. She gives the soul a taste for all that is of God so that in her company one loses the taste for the comforts of mere creatures. She delights the spirit by the brilliance of her light; she fills the heart with joy, satisfaction, and unutterable peace, even in the midst of hardship and in the most disagreeable trials—as Paul attested when he said: "*In all our hardship I am overflowing with joy*" (2 Cor 7:4).

*Entering my house, though I be alone, I find a sweet repose with her, for her conversation has in it nothing disagreeable, nor her company anything tedious, but only contentment and joy* (Ws 8:16).

And not only in my own house and in communion with her *did I find joy, but everywhere, in all places and in all things, because she walked before me* (Ws 7:12). *There is a true and holy 'delight in her friendship'* (Ws 8:18), which takes the place of the joys and pleasures one could find among creatures—who, after all, offer only the illusion of pleasure, and often afflict the spirit besides.

**99.** 4) When Eternal Wisdom gives herself to a soul, she communicates also all the gifts of the Holy Spirit and all the important virtues to an eminent degree:

- the *theological* virtues: a living faith, a firm hope, a burning charity;

- the *cardinal* virtues: a well-ordered temperance, a perfect prudence, a flawless justice, an invincible strength;
- the *moral* virtues: perfect religion, profound humility, irresistible gentleness, blind obedience, complete detachment, continuous mortification, sublime prayer, etc.

These are the great virtues and heavenly gifts that the Holy Spirit describes:

> *"If it be uprightness that you desire, virtues are the fruit of her labors, since it is she who teaches temperance and prudence, justice and fortitude"* (Ws 8:7).

**100.** 5) Finally, *since there is nothing more active than Wisdom* (Ws 7:24) she does not allow her friends to sink into mediocrity or negligence. She fires them up. She inspires them with great projects for the glory of God and for the salvation of souls. And to make them more worthy, she sees that they have occasions of combat, and she disciplines them with contradictions and reversals in almost everything they undertake.

Sometimes she allows Satan to tempt them, and sometimes she allows the world to lie about them and reject them. Sometimes she permits their enemies to overcome and subdue them, and sometimes their friends and relatives to abandon and betray them. At one point she will arrange that they lose their possessions; at another time she might visit them with an illness; now it may be a stinging insult that comes, or again it may be a sorrow, a blow to the heart. In short, she tests these friends of hers by every possible way as gold is tested in fire.[3]

> *But their affliction was light and their reward will be great, because God tempted them and found them worthy. He tested them like gold in the furnace; received them like the sacrifice of the holocaust; and regarded them favorably when their time came due* (Ws 3:4-6).

> *Wisdom protected her servants from their ordeals. She brought them success in their labors, and gave them full return for all their efforts; she stood by them against grasping oppressors, and she made them rich. She preserved them from their enemies, and saved them from the traps that were set for them. In an arduous struggle she awarded them the prize, to teach them that (wisdom) is stronger than all* (Ws 10:10-12).

**101.** A story is told in the life of Blessed Henry Suso, a Dominican friar. In his burning desire

3 Cf. Za 13: 9; Mt 3: 3

to possess Eternal Wisdom, he offered several times to suffer for her sake any torment that might be required in order to obtain her friendship. One day he said to himself, "Hey! Do you not know that lovers are willing to embrace a thousand sufferings for the sake of the one they love? All-night prayer is a pleasure for them; even fatigue is agreeable; and work is a relaxation—if only the lover can feel that his beloved will take note of his efforts and be pleased. If ordinary humans go to such lengths to please a mere pile of compost, would you not blush with shame to hesitate in your pursuit of Wisdom?" "No, O Eternal Wisdom," Suso declared, "I will not hold anything back! I shall face both thickets and thorns—any kind of obstacle, in fact—so long as I finally arrive at your dwelling place. Even if my body and soul should have to become the objects of a thousand torments, still I will value your favor above everything, and you will be the absolute queen of my heart."

**102.** A few days later while traveling, Suso fell into the hands of robbers who beat him up and reduced him to such a terrible state that even they were moved to pity. Seeing himself so abandoned and helpless, Henry fell into a dark depression. Forgetting his resolve to have courage no matter what happened, he started to weep and asked why God should so hurt him. With this thought in mind, he fainted. The next morning near dawn, he heard a voice speaking reproachfully to him: "So this is our soldier who crosses mountains, climbs rocks, raids castles, and kills and dismembers his enemies. This is the way he is on good days when things are going smoothly; but when difficulties arise, his courage fails, and he can't even find his arms and legs to pull himself up. He is a lion in good times, but he is a frightened gazelle when put to the test. Well, Wisdom doesn't offer her friendship to the faint-hearted or to cowards."

Upon hearing this rebuke, Blessed Henry confessed how mistaken he had been to be so greatly distressed; at the same time he asked Wisdom to allow him to weep, so that he could release some of the heaviness of his heart. "No, no," a voice replied, "the heavenly hosts would lose respect for you if you were to give in to your tears like a child or a woman; wipe your eyes and put on a happy face."

**103.** So the cross is both the destiny and the reward of those who desire Wisdom, or who already possess her. But, of course, this kind mistress, "*who numbers, weighs, and measures all things*" (Ws 11:20), tailors her crosses according to the strength of her loved ones. And even more, she so perfumes these crosses with the sweet aroma of her presence that they act as reminders of her sweet company.

### The Excellence of Charity

(Canticle 5:40, 43-47)

A thousand times my heart desires you
Love divine, come to me.
To be without you is a martyrdom,
Come then impart to me your law.

Forgive, O charity divine,
My defiance and my coolness.
That is past, I open my breast
To your charm and your ardor.

By Mary's womb,
By the merits of Jesus,
Come to me I beg you,
No more shall I rebuff you.

Divine Jesus, love supreme,
You alone I love on earth,
I love you and call accursed
Those who love you not.

Yes, dear love, I love you,
Not for fear of punishment,
Nor even for the reward,
But only for you alone.

Dear Bridegroom, I embrace you.
All I am I give to you,
It is right for me to do so,
For you were first to embrace me.

## Chapter 9

### Eternal Wisdom's Incarnation and Earthly Life

104. IT WAS in the high council of the Holy Trinity that Wisdom, the Eternal Word, made his decision. He would become human, so that fallen humanity might be restored. One might imagine that Adam himself knew of this decision; in any case, scripture tells us that the patriarchs of old were aware of the promise that the Word would take human flesh for the redemption of the world.

Thus we can see why, for the length of the four thousand years from the creation of the world to the Incarnation (calculated in Jewish time), all the saints of the Old Law were praying for the coming of the Messiah. With sighs of deepest desire they uttered their pleas, crying out: *"O clouds, rain down the Just One! O Earth, bud forth the Savior!"*[1] "O Wisdom, who proceeded from the mouth of the Most High, come bring us deliverance!"

But even their prayers and sacrifices were not powerful enough to draw down Eternal Wisdom, the Son of God, from his dwelling in the bosom of the Father. They lifted their arms towards heaven, but their reach was not long enough to grasp the throne of the Most High. Though they made offerings unceasingly, even

1 Antiphon used during Advent as opening antiphon for the 4th Sunday.

of their hearts, these were not sufficient to merit the grace of all graces.

**105.** Finally, the time appointed for the redemption of humankind arrived. Eternal Wisdom made herself a home, a dwelling worthy of herself: *"Wisdom has fashioned a dwelling place for herself"* (Pr 9:1). She created and formed the divine Mary, in the womb of St. Anne, with greater pleasure than she had taken in creating the universe. It is impossible to express, on the one hand, the wondrous communication that the Holy Trinity made to this lovely creature, and on the other, the fidelity with which she responded to the grace of the Creator.

**106.** The free-flowing waters of the infinite goodness of God, which had been so rudely dammed up by the sins of humankind since the world's beginning, were now unleashed to pour out spontaneously into the heart of Mary. Eternal Wisdom gave her all the graces that Adam and his descendants would have received if they had remained in original justice. In the words of a saint, the fullness of divinity was poured out upon Mary to the full extent that a mere creature was capable of receiving it. O Mary, Masterpiece of the Most High, O Miracle of Eternal Wisdom, O Unsurpassed Marvel of the Almighty One, O Bottomless Vessel of Grace! I say boldly with all the saints, that none but the

Creator knows the height, the breadth, and the depth of the grace that he has infused in you.

**107.** In fourteen short years of life,[2] the divine Mary received such abundant gifts of grace and wisdom, and responded with such perfect faithfulness to divine love, that she attracted the admiration not only of the angels, but of God himself. The immeasurable depth of her humility charmed him; her divine purity enticed him; her lively faith and her frequent and loving prayers captivated him: Wisdom's capacity for love was conquered by Mary's loving advances. "O how great indeed was the love of Mary that it could conquer the Most High."[3] It is indeed astonishing that Divine Wisdom desired to descend from the bosom of the Father into the womb of a Virgin, so as to lie there *among the lilies*[4] of her purity, and abandon herself entirely to Mary, thus acquiring human nature in her. To this end, she, Wisdom dispatched the angel Gabriel to greet Mary on Wisdom's behalf, to indicate that Mary had won her heart, and that she desired to become incarnate in her, provided that Mary gave her consent. The Archangel fulfilled his mission. Having assured Mary that she would remain a

2 These are two Christian apocrypha and not the gospel of Luke which gauges the age of Mary at the time of the Annunciation: Gospel of pseudo Mt 8:1, Book of the Birth of Mary 7:3.

3 Source uncertain.

4 Canticle 2:16:6, 2

virgin while becoming a mother, he won from her even in the face of her profound humility the 'yes' that the Holy Trinity along with all the angels, and indeed the entire universe, had been awaiting for so long. Bowing deeply before her Creator, Mary said: "*Behold the handmaiden of the Lord; be it done to me according to your word*" (Lk 1:38).

**108.** At the moment when Mary gave her consent to be the Mother of God, see how many miracles took place. The Holy Spirit formed from the pure blood of her heart a little body, perfectly structured; and he created the most perfect soul that he had ever made. Eternal Wisdom, the Son of God, united himself personally and truly to this body and to this soul. Thus there came about the great marvel of heaven and earth, the unbelievably generous excess of the love of God: "*The Word was made flesh*" (Jn 1:14). Eternal Wisdom becomes incarnate. God becomes man without ceasing to be God; this God is called Jesus Christ, which means Savior.

**Let us now contemplate an overview of his life.**

**109.** 1) He wanted to be born of a married woman, but one who was in fact a virgin. Perhaps he wanted to avoid the shameful label of illegitimacy, or perhaps there were other important reasons for his choice, such as have been mentioned by the Fathers of the Church. His conception was announced to the Holy Virgin by the angel Gabriel, as we have just told it. In this way, he became a child of Adam, but without inheriting Adam's sin. This event took place on a Friday, the 25th of March.

**110.** 2) On the 25th of December, the Savior of the world was born in the town of Bethlehem, in a poor stable, where a manger served as his cradle. An angel announced to the shepherds who were keeping watch over their flocks in the fields, that the Savior was born, and instructed them to go and adore him in Bethlehem. At the same time, they heard heavenly music, angels who were singing: *"Glory be to God in the highest, and on earth peace to people of good will"* (Lk 2:14).

**111.** 3) On the eighth day he was circumcised, according to the Law of Moses to which he was not really subject, and from heaven he was given the name Jesus. Three Wise Men from the East came to adore him, alerted by the appearance of an extraordinary star that guided them to Bethlehem. This feast is called Epiphany, *i.e.,* the manifestation of God celebrated on the 6th of January.

**112.** 4) He wanted to present himself as an offering to the temple forty days after his birth, in full observance of all that the Law of Moses required for the redemption of the firstborn. A short while later, the angel warned Joseph, the husband of the Holy Virgin, to take the infant Jesus and his mother, and to flee into Egypt, so as to avoid the wrath of Herod. This Joseph did. Some authors maintain that Our Lord was in Egypt for two years; others say three; others, such as Baronius, say as many as eight. His presence sanctified the whole country so that it became worthy later to be populated by the holy Desert Fathers, as history records. Eusebius says that when Jesus entered the region, the demons took flight; and St. Athanasius affirms that the idols fell down before Him.

**113.** 5) At twelve years of age, the Son of God led a dialogue in the assembly of the rabbis, displaying so much wisdom that he earned the admiration of all his hearers. Following this incident, scripture is silent until his baptism, which took place in the thirtieth year of his life. After that he retired to the desert, where he fasted for forty days without eating or drinking. There he struggled with the devil over whom he was victorious.

**114.** 6) After that he began to preach in Judea, to call the apostles, and to work all the wondrous miracles that the sacred scriptures record. It is enough to note that in the third year of his preaching, the thirty-third year of his life,

Jesus raised Lazarus; that he made his triumphal entry into Jerusalem on the 29th of March, and that on the second day of April, which was a Thursday, the 14th day of the month of Nissan, he celebrated the Passover with his disciples, washed their feet, and instituted the blessed sacrament of the Eucharist under the form of bread and wine.

**115.** 7) On the evening of this day, he was captured by his enemies, who were led to him by the traitor Judas. The next day, the third of April, in spite of the fact that it was a religious holiday, he was condemned to death after being beaten, crowned with thorns, and utterly humiliated. On the same day, he was taken to Calvary and nailed on a cross between two criminals. And that is the story of how the God of Innocence chose to die the most shameful of deaths, and to endure the torment destined for a thief named Barabbas, whom the Jews preferred over him. The Fathers of the Church suggest that Jesus Christ was attached to the cross with four nails, and that his body was supported by a kind of wooden seat that extended out from the middle of the cross.

**116.** 8) After three excruciating hours, the Savior of the world expired in his thirty-third year. Joseph of Arimathea had the courage to request his body from Pilate, and put it in a tomb newly cut out of the rock. One should not overlook the effects that nature suffered upon the death of its Creator. Its grief was manifested in extraordinary signs that appeared the moment Jesus expired. He rose on the 5th of April and appeared several times to his holy Mother and to his disciples during forty days, until Thursday the 14th of May, when he led his disciples to the top of the Mount of Olives. There in their presence, he rose by his own power into the heavens at the right hand of his Father leaving the traces of his sacred footsteps upon the earth.

## Noel of Spiritual Souls
(Canticle 64:1-3, 5-6)

In order to save people, God
Decided on marvelous mystery;
He becomes what we are,
Making us become what He is.

The most high Lord lowered Himself
To raise us to heaven.
He came into our lowliness
To grant us His glorious life.

He became powerless
To make us all-powerful,
He became an infant
To make us immortal.

To break our chains, He was bound Himself.
He took on our sufferings
To give us His pleasures and riches.

God became like us
Through infinite love;
It is right and fitting
To imitate and resemble Him.

## Chapter 10

### Incarnate Wisdom's Charming Beauty and Inexpressible Sweetness

**117.** SINCE Wisdom took on our human nature for the sole purpose of charming the human heart and winning us both to intimacy in her friendship and to imitation of her, it was her pleasure to adorn herself with all possible graces and attractive qualities. She displays her attractiveness sweetly and kindly, in the way that is most likely to touch us. This she does in a completely appropriate and harmonious way.

**118.** As we contemplate Wisdom in her very origin, we see that her essential qualities are tender compassion and sweetness. She is the gift of the Eternal Father's love, and the evidence of the love of the Holy Spirit. She is given out of love, and fashioned by love. *"God so loved the world that he gave his only begotten Son"* (Jn 3:16). You might say that she is herself entirely love, the very love of the Father and of the Spirit.

He, Wisdom (Incarnate), was born of the sweetest, as well as the most tender and beautiful of all mothers, Mary. To understand the sweetness of Jesus, I advise you first to appreciate the sweetness of Mary, his Mother, whom, of course, he resembles by temperament. Jesus is the child of Mary, and so we see in him no arrogance, no cruelty, and no ugliness. Indeed, by nature he possesses the perfection of divine qualities infinitely more than his Mother, since he is Eternal Wisdom, and the very essence of beauty and sweetness.

**119.** The prophets who were given a prevision of Wisdom Incarnate, referred to him as "mother sheep" and "gentle lamb" (Jn 11:19). They prophesied his gentleness: *"He would not crush a bent reed, nor snuff out a smoking candlewick"* (Is 42:3).[1] This means that however much a poor sinner might be bent, broken, half-blind, or all but lost by his sins with one foot in hell, as it were, Jesus would not entirely abandon him, unless he, the sinner forced him to. St. John the Baptist, after nearly thirty years of austerities in the desert preparing to attain to the love and knowledge of Wisdom, no sooner saw him than he cried out to his disciples, proclaiming: *"Behold the Lamb of God, who takes away the sins of the world"* (Jn 1:29). He didn't say, as it seems he should have: "There is the Most High; there is the King of Glory; there is the Almighty." Instead, recognizing His essence more profoundly than anyone else before or since, he said: "There is the Lamb of God," there is Eternal Wisdom who to charm our

1 Cf. Mt 12:20

hearts and dissolve our sins integrated within himself all the sweetness of God and of humanity, of heaven and of earth.

**120.** What does the very name of Jesus mean to us the name that is proper to Incarnate Wisdom? Does it not suggest a burning love, a limitless charity, an irresistible sweetness? Jesus, Savior, he who saves humankind, whose essential nature is to love and save humankind!

> No song is sweeter,
> no sound more joyous,
> No thought more soothing,
> than the name of Jesus, Son of God.[2]

O how sweet is the name of Jesus in the ears and in the heart of a predestined soul. It is honey in the mouth, melody in the ears, and joy in the heart![3]

**121.** "Jesus is sweet in his facial expression, sweet in his words, and sweet in his manner and behavior."[4]

This gentle Savior has a countenance so open and kindly that it captivated the eyes and hearts of all those who beheld him. The shepherds who came to see him in the stable were so taken by the grace and sweetness of his face

2 Hymn attributed to St. Bernard

3 St. Bernard

4 St. Augustine

that they stayed for days, beside themselves in rapturous contemplation.

No sooner had the three stately kings begun to sense the love in the expression of this beautiful child, than, forgetting their royal status, they were moved to kneel down humbly in front of his manger. How many times did they say to each other: "Friend, how good it is to be here! In our own palaces there is no pleasure to compare with what we are feeling right now in this stable, in the presence of the divine child."

Jesus was still quite young when children and people in distress came from all over the neighboring area to see him, and to be uplifted by him. They said to each other: "Let's go see little Jesus, the beautiful child of Mary." The beauty and the majesty of his facial expression, said St. John Chrysostom, were at once so gentle and so full of authority that those who knew him could not keep from loving him. It is even said that faraway kings, hearing news of his extraordinary grace, wanted to have his picture. There is a legend that Our Lord himself sent one as a special favor to King Abgar.[5] Some authors state that the Roman soldiers and Jewish prosecutors covered his face so that they would

5 According to a legend, the king Abdess of Edesse had sent an emissary asking Jesus to come to heal him. The latter dictated a letter to a scribe who was also a painter and sent the king Jesus' response and his portrait.

be able more easily to beat him and abuse him. For there came out from his eyes and from his face a shining power that was so kind and yet so forceful that it disarmed even the cruelest of those who looked upon him.

122. Jesus is gentle in his speech. While he was living on the earth, he won to himself every person he met by the sweetness of his words. As the prophets had foretold, he was never heard shouting too loudly, nor engaging in heated dispute: "*He does not cry out or raise his voice; His voice is not heard in the streets*" (Is 42:2). All those of good will who listened to him were so affected by the words of life that flowed from his lips that they exclaimed, "*No one has ever spoken as this one*" (Jn 7:46). Even the enemies who opposed him were taken by surprise with the eloquence and wisdom of his words. They wondered: "*Where does his wisdom come from?*" (Mk 6:2; Mt 15:34). Never had a human being spoken with such gentleness and grace.

Thousands of poor people left their homes and families to go and hear him even in the desert. Sometimes they spent days without drinking or eating, satisfied with savoring his words. It was by the sweetness of his words that he drew to himself a following, especially of the apostles; that he cured the sick, even those considered incurable; and that he was able to console the most afflicted. For the grieving Mary Magdalene it was enough that he said one word, "Mary,"[6] to fill her cup to the brim with consolation and joy.

6 Cf. Jn 20:16

# Chapter 11

## Incarnate Wisdom's Gentle Speech and Behavior

123. JESUS is gentle in his actions and in the way he lived his entire life: "*He did everything well*" (Mk 7:37). All that Jesus Christ did, he did exactly right with such wisdom, holiness, and kindness that none could find fault with his conduct. Let us observe this gentleness that filled and flooded Wisdom's every action.

124. The poor and the little children followed him everywhere as though he were one of them. They found in this dear Savior so much simplicity, good will, understanding, and real concern, that they crowded around to get near him. One day when he was preaching in the street, the children, who loved to accompany him, happened to crowd around him from behind. The Apostles who were closest to the Lord pushed them back. Jesus noticed that, and reprimanded his Apostles, saying: "*Let the little children come to me*" (Mk 10:14). When they came to him, he took them in his arms and blessed them. How gentle and kind he was to them!

Poor people too could see that he was dressed like other poor folk, and likewise that his manner was simple, *i.e.* without pretense. So they enjoyed his company, taking up his defense when the rich and the status-conscious spoke out against him and made him the target of their opposition. For his part he was happy to offer the poor his support and his blessings on every possible occasion.

**125.** But who could describe the sweetness that sinners especially felt in the presence of Jesus! How kindly did he treat the sinner Magdalene; with what understanding and regard did he convert the Samaritan woman! With what mercy did he pardon the woman taken in adultery! What openness he showed in choosing to eat with public sinners in order to win their hearts! Did not his enemies take advantage of his kindness in accusing him of breaking the Law of Moses, and in wickedly calling him the friend of sinners and publicans? With what kindliness and humility did he try to win the heart of Judas when he was on the point of betraying him, washing his feet and calling him friend! Finally, with what charity did he not ask pardon of God his Father for his very tormentors, whom he excused on the grounds of their ignorance!

**126.** Indeed, how sweet, how loving, and lovely is Jesus, Wisdom Incarnate! She is beautiful in eternity, for she is the splendor of the Father, the spotless mirror and image of his goodness, more beautiful than the sun and more brilliant than light itself! She is beautiful too in the dimension of time, for she was fashioned by the Holy Spirit to be pure, immaculate, and full of grace.

Her sweetness was displayed during the whole of her earthly life, for she charmed the eyes and hearts of humans. It still shines out, for her sweetness is the glory of the Angels. It persists too in her relationship with humanity, towards whom she remains always tender and kind. But especially does it persist in her relationship to sinners. In her visible form she came to seek them, and she continues to seek them invisibly every day!

**127.** Let us not imagine that Jesus in his triumphant and glorious state is any less appealing and approachable than before; on the contrary, glory in a certain way perfects his gracious kindness. For he desires less to appear victorious than to pardon; he longs less to display the riches of his glory than to show the excess of his mercy.

**128.** In the accounts that we read of Incarnate Wisdom's appearances to her friends, we observe that she did not usually show herself in a setting of thunder and lightning, but in a sweet and kindly way. She did not assume the majesty and sovereignty of the God of Hosts, but rather the tenderness of a spouse and the gentleness of a friend. She sometimes allowed herself to be seen in the Eucharist; but I don't remember any account where she appeared in a form other than as a lovely child.

**129.** Some time ago an unfortunate person, enraged that he had lost his money in a game of chance, drew his sword against heaven, and cursed the Lord for the loss of his money. Surprise! Instead of thunder and fire raining down upon him, a little piece of paper floated gently around him. Astonished, he caught the paper, opened it, and read: "Lord, have mercy on me." The sword fell from his hands. He was touched to his depths; he fell down and cried out for mercy.

**130.** St. Dennis the Areopagite reports another such story. A bishop named Carpas, having invested considerable effort in converting a person who worshiped false idols, learned a short time later that a former friend of the new convert had persuaded him to renounce his newfound faith. All night long Carpas complained to God in his prayers and demanded revenge for the injury done to the divine majesty. As his zealous prayers reached a heated peak, he suddenly saw the earth open up; then he saw swaying on the very edge of hell this same apostate and his idolatrous friend whom the demons were trying to grab. He lifted his eyes and saw heaven open, and Jesus Christ coming to him with a multitude of Angels saying: "Carpas, you ask for revenge; you do not know me. Do you realize what you are asking me, or how much sinners have cost me? Why do you want me to abandon them? I love them, and I am ready to die a second time for any one of them, if it should be necessary." Then Our Lord approached Carpas, and baring His shoulders said. "Carpas, if it is revenge you want, strike me instead of these poor sinners."

**131.** After all these examples, shall we not love this Eternal Wisdom who has loved us and continues to love us more than her own life, whose beauty and sweetness surpass all that is most beautiful and satisfying in heaven and on earth?

**132.** It is reported in the Life of Blessed Henry Suso, that one day Wisdom, whom he desired ardently, appeared to him in this manner: She was surrounded with a bright translucent cloud, and seated on a throne of ivory. Radiating from her face and eyes was brightness like the rays of the noonday sun. Her crown represented eternity; her robe suggested happiness; her word was loving kindness; and her embrace represented the fulfilment of all the blessed. What surprised Henry most was that sometimes she appeared as a young girl who was a miracle of heaven and earth in beauty, and sometimes it was a young man he saw, whose face seemed to shine with all the glories of creation. At one moment he saw her with her head lifted high above the clouds, while her feet were rooted in the depths of the earth. Sometimes he saw her from afar, and sometimes approaching near. Sometimes she was majestic, and at other times humble and kind, sweet and full of tenderness towards those who approached her. Once when she appeared in this way, she turned towards him, and smiling in a friendly way, said: "My son, give me your heart!" At that moment Henry flung himself at her feet and made the gift of his heart to her once and for all.

Following the example of this holy person, let us make Eternal and Incarnate Wisdom a gift of our heart which is all that she asks of us.

**Loving Excesses of the Sacred Heart**

(Canticle 41:1, 19, 28, 34-36)

Let us go deep within the Temple,
Let us enter this marvelous Heart,
So that we may love as it does,
Let us gaze at its excess of love.

By the sovereign meekness
Of his most tender and gentle Heart,
He converted the Magdalene
And shielded her from others.

Alas! he is taken and bound,
Overwhelmed with a thousand blows,
They hail him, they crucify him,
His Heart is always so gentle.

His Father grants his prayer,
Behold! His side is pierced,
And from the gash, a river flows
Of water, blood and love.

Finally, the furnace opens up!
Finally this great Heart unlocks;
Finally the reason is clear
Why Jesus has so suffered.

By piercing his Heart, he is consoled;
The passageway carved by the lance
For his Heart's devouring fire,
Leads straight to the heart of the sinner.

# CHAPTER 12

## Incarnate Wisdom's Core Teachings: What We Must Believe and Do in Order to Be Saved[1]

**133.**

1. *THOSE who want to become a follower of mine, let them renounce themselves and take up their cross every day and follow me* (Lk 9:23).

2. *Those who love me will keep my word, and my Father will love them, and we shall come to them and make a home in them* (Jn 14:23).

3. *So then, if you are bringing your offering to the altar, and there you remember that your brother or sister has anything against you, leave your offering there before the altar; go and be reconciled with your brother or sister first, and then come back and present your offering* (Mt 5:23-24).

1 The first forty-nine "oracles" were taken almost literally from A. Bonnefons, S.J., a small book of life which teaches how to live well and to pray well (1st edition, 1650). But this edition, augmented by twelve evangelical oracles as well as the series of eight beatitudes found in Matthew, serves the purpose of Montfort admirably. He thus gives us a glimpse of the exceptional, and often paradoxical, wisdom of Jesus, and he suggests to the reader to welcome the whole of the Gospels as the most beautiful and the greatest of wisdoms, because there, there is "greater than Solomon" (Lk 11:31).

**134.**

4. *Anyone who comes to me and does not hate his father, mother, wife, children, brothers, sisters, yes and his own life too, cannot be my disciple* (Lk 14:26).

5. *And everyone who has left houses, brothers, sisters, father, mother, children or land for the sake of my name will receive a hundred times as much, and also inherit eternal life* (Mt 19:29).

6. *If you want to be perfect, go and sell your possessions and give the money to the poor, and you will have treasure in heaven; and come follow me* (Mt 19:21).

**135.**

7. *It is not anyone who says to me Lord, Lord, who will enter the kingdom of heaven, but the one who does the will of my Father in heaven* (Mt 7:21).

8. *Therefore, anyone who listens to these words of mine and acts on them will be like a sensible person who built their house on rock* (Mt 7:24).

9. *In truth I tell you, unless you change and become like little children, you will never enter the kingdom of heaven* (Mt 18:3).

10. *Shoulder my yoke and learn from me, for I am gentle and humble of heart, and you shall find rest for your souls* (Mt 11:29).

**136.**

11. *And when you pray, do not imitate the hypocrites: they love to say their prayers standing up in the synagogues and at the street corners for people to see them* (Mt 6:5).

12. *In your prayers, do not engage in useless repetition as the gentiles do, for they think that by using many words they will make themselves heard. For your Father knows what you need before you ask him* (Mt 6:7-8).

13. *And when you stand in prayer, forgive whatever you have against anybody, so that your Father in heaven may forgive you your failings too* (Mk 11:25).

14. *I tell you, everything you ask and pray for, believe that you have it already and it will be yours* (Mk 11:24).

**137.**

15. *When you are fasting, do not put on a gloomy look as the hypocrites do; they*

*go about looking unsightly to let people know they are fasting. I tell you they have already had their reward* (Mt 6:16).

**138.**

16. *I tell you, there will be more rejoicing in heaven over one sinner repenting than over ninety-nine upright people who have no need of repentance* (Lk 15:7).

17. *I have not come to call the upright, but sinners to repentance* (Lk 5:32).

**139.**

18. *Blessed are those who are persecuted in the cause of uprightness; the kingdom of heaven is theirs* (Mt 5:10).

19. *Blessed are you when people hate you or drive you out or abuse you or denounce your name as criminal on account of the Son of Man. Rejoice when that day comes and dance for joy. Look! Your reward will be great in heaven* (Lk 6:22-23).

20. *If the world hates you, you must realize that it hated me before it hated you. If you belonged to the world,*

*the world would love you as its own; but because you do not belong to the world, because my choice of you has drawn you out of the world, that is why the world hates you* (Jn 15:18-19).

**140.**

21. *Come to me all you who labor and are burdened, and I will give you rest* (Mt 11:28).

22. *I am the living bread which has come down from heaven. Anyone who eats this bread will live forever. And the bread that I shall give is my flesh for the life of the world* (Jn 6:51-52).

23. *My flesh is real food and my blood is real drink. Whoever eats my flesh and drinks my blood lives in me, and I live in that person* (Jn 6:55-56).

**141.**

24. *You will be hated universally on account of my name, but not a hair of your head will be lost* (Lk 21:17-18).

**142.**

25. *No one can be the slave of two masters. That person will either love the first*

*and hate the second, or be attached to the first and despise the second. You cannot be the slave of God and of money* (Mt 6:24).

**143.**

26. *For from the heart come evil intentions: murder, adultery, fornication, theft, perjury, slander. These are the things that make a person unclean. But eating with unwashed hands does not make anyone unclean* (Mt 15:19-20).

27. *Good people draw good things from their store of goodness, from the treasure of their heart, and evil people draw evil things from their store of evil* (Mt 12:35).

**144.**

28. *Once the hand is laid on the plough, no one who looks back is fit for the kingdom of God* (Lk 9:62).

29. *Every hair on your head has been counted. There is no need to be afraid: you are worth more than many sparrows* (Lk 12:7).

30. *For God sent his Son into the world not to judge the world, but so that through him the world might be saved* (Jn 3:17).

**145.**

31. *Indeed everyone who does wrong hates the light and avoids it for fear of his actions being shown* (Jn 3:20).

32. *God is spirit, and those who worship must worship in spirit and truth* (Jn 4:24).

33. *It is the spirit who gives life. The flesh has nothing to offer. The words I have spoken to you are spirit and they are life* (Jn 6:63).

34. *In all truth I tell you, whoever commits a sin is a slave. Now a slave has no permanent standing in the household, but the son belongs to it forever* (Jn 8:34-35).

35. *Anyone who is trustworthy in little things is trustworthy in great; anyone who is dishonest in little things is dishonest in great* (Lk 16:10).

36. *It is easier for heaven and earth to disappear than for one little iota to drop out of the law without being fulfilled* (Lk 16:17).

37. *So your light must shine in people's sight, so that, seeing your good works, they may give praise to your Father in heaven* (Mt 5:16).

**146.**

38. *For I tell you, if your uprightness does not surpass that of the scribes and Pharisees, you will never get into the kingdom of heaven* (Mt 5:20).

39. *If your right eye should be your downfall, tear it out and throw it away; for it will do you less harm to lose one part of yourself than to have your whole body thrown into hell* (Mt 5:29).

40. *The kingdom of heaven has been subjected to violence and the violent are taking it by storm* (Mt 11:12).

41. *Do not store up treasures for yourselves on earth, where moth and woodworm and thieves can break in and steal. But store up treasures for yourselves in heaven, where neither moth nor woodworm destroy them and thieves cannot break in and steal* (Mt 6:19-20).

42. *Do not judge and you will not be judged because the judgments you give are the judgments you will get, and the standard you use will be the standard used for you* (Mt 7:1-2).

**147.**

43. Be*ware of the false prophets who come to you disguised as sheep but underneath are ravenous wolves. You will be able to tell them by their fruits* (Mt 7:15-16).

44. *See that you never despise any of these little ones, for I tell you that their angels in heaven are continually in the presence of my Father in heaven* (Mt 18:10).

45. *Stay awake because you do not know the day or the hour* (Mt 25:13).

**148.**

46. *Do not be afraid of those who kill the body and after that can do no more. I will tell you whom to fear: fear him who, after he has killed, has the power to cast into hell* (Lk 12:4-5).

47. *This is why I am telling you not to worry about your life and what you are to eat, nor about your body and how you are to clothe it. Your Father well knows your needs* (Lk 12:22, 30).

48. *Nothing is hidden but it will be made clear; nothing is secret but it will be*

*made known and brought to light* (Lk 8:17).

**149.**

49. *Anyone who wants to become great among you must be your servant; and anyone who wants to be first among you must be your slave* (Mt 20:26-27).

50. *How hard it is for those who have riches to enter the kingdom of God!* (Mk 10:23).

51. *It is easier for a camel to pass through the eye of a needle than for someone rich to enter the kingdom of God* (Lk 18:25).

52. *I say this to you: love your enemies and pray for those who persecute you* (Mt 5:44).

53. *But alas for you rich, you have your consolation now* (Lk 6:24).

**150.**

54. *Enter by the narrow gate, since the road that leads to destruction is wide and spacious, and many take it; but it is a narrow gate and a hard road that leads to life, and only a few find it* (Mt 7:13-14).

55. *The last will be first, and the first last. For many are called, but few are chosen* (Mt 20:16). *There is more happiness in giving than in receiving* (Acts 20:35).

56. *If someone hits you on the right cheek, offer him the other as well; if someone wishes to go to law with you to get your tunic, let him have your cloak as well* (Mt 5:39-40).

57. *Pray continually and never lose heart* (Lk 18:1). *Stay awake and pray not to be put to the test* (Mt 26:41).

58. *Give alms from what you have, and everything will be clean for you* (Lk 11:41).

59. *Everyone who raises himself up will be humbled, and the one who humbles himself will be raised up* (Lk 14:11).

60. *If your hand or your foot should be your downfall, cut it off and throw it away; it is better for you to enter into life crippled or lame, than to have two hands or two feet and be thrown into eternal fire. And if your eye should be your downfall, tear it out and throw it away: it is better for you to enter into*

***life with one eye, than to have two eyes and be thrown into the hell of fire*** **(Mt 18:8-9).**

**151.**

**61. The Eight Beatitudes**

1. Blessed are the poor in spirit; the kingdom of heaven is theirs.
2. Blessed are the gentle; they shall have the earth as inheritance.
3. Blessed are those who mourn; they shall be comforted.
4. Blessed are those who hunger and thirst for uprightness; they shall have their fill.
5. Blessed are the merciful; for they shall have mercy shown them.
6. Blessed are the pure in heart; they shall see God.
7. Blessed are the peacemakers; they shall be recognized as children of God.
8. Blessed are those who are persecuted in the cause of uprightness; the kingdom of heaven is theirs **(Mt 5:3-10).**

**152.**

62. *Jesus exclaimed, "I give you thanks, Father, Lord of heaven and of earth, for hiding these things from the learned and the clever and revealing them to the little ones. Yes, Father, for that is what it pleased you to do"* (Mt 11:25-26).

**153.** This is a short summary of the important truths that Eternal Wisdom came to teach us on this earth. She herself practiced them first, so as to rescue us from our blindness and keep us from getting lost along the way of our sinfulness.

- Happy are those who have insight into the truth of these teachings.
- Happier still are those who submit to these teachings in faith.
- Happiest of all are those who, having faith in them, follow them and teach them to others; "for they will shine like the stars in heaven for all eternity" (Dn 12:3).

## Chapter 13

### The Sorrows That Incarnate Wisdom Chose to Undergo on Our Behalf

**154.** OF ALL the reasons I can think of that move us to the love of Jesus Christ, Incarnate Wisdom, the strongest, in my opinion, lies in the sorrows he was willing to undergo to show his love for us. "There is one motive," says St. Bernard, "that takes precedence over all others and moves me most deeply to the love of Jesus Christ: that is, O gentle Jesus, the chalice of bitterness that you drank for us and the work of our redemption that so touches our hearts. Indeed, this supreme gift of your love and the incredible evidence of it that you gave us, easily wins our response. By your sufferings you attract us more sweetly; you discipline us more suitably; you bind us more closely; and you move us more powerfully." Bernard then summarizes the reason in these few brief words: "Our dear Savior has worked and suffered so much to redeem us. How many the sufferings and how great the anguish that he endured for us!"

**155.** In order to grasp clearly the limitless extent of Wisdom's love, we need to look closely at all the circumstances woven together in his enormous suffering.

The *first* of these is the supreme nature of the person who suffers. The person of Jesus elevates the sufferings of his passion to the level of infinity. If God had sent a seraph or an angel of the lowest order to become human and die for us, this would doubtless have been something marvelous and deserving of our eternal gratitude. But that the Creator of heaven and earth, the only Son of God, Eternal Wisdom herself should come to give her life—that is an incredible thing! For compared to her the lives of all angels, all humans, and all creatures put together are infinitely less than the life of a housefly compared to the lives of all the kings and rulers of the world! What an excess of charity are we given to behold in this mystery, and how great must be our astonishment and gratitude!

**156.** The *second* circumstance is the nature of the persons for whom Christ suffers. These are humans—lowly creatures—who have made themselves his enemies, from whom he had nothing to fear, nor anything to hope for. Once in a while we hear of people who have died for their friends; but shall we ever meet anyone but the Son of God who has died for his enemy? *"Jesus Christ made visible the love he bears for us by dying for us, even while we were still sinners, and so in a state of enmity with him"* (Rm 5:8-9).

**157.** The *third* circumstance is to be found in the extent, the acuteness, and the duration of his sufferings. As to the extent: his sufferings were so great that he has been called the Man of Sorrows. His wounds extend from the soles of his feet to the crown of his head, so that there is no sound place in him. This tremendous lover of our souls has suffered in every possible way: within and without, in his body and in his soul.

**158.** He suffered from material poverty. We can pass briefly over the poverty of his birth and of his life as a refugee in Egypt, and indeed the poverty of his whole life. We contemplate him now in the privations he suffered during his passion where we see him stripped even of his garments by the soldiers who divided them up; finally, we see him nailed naked to the Cross, without even a rag to cover him.

**159.** He suffered in his honor and reputation, becoming the target of all manner of insults: called blasphemer, rabble-rouser, drunkard, glutton, and one possessed by demons. He was insulted in his wisdom by being called an ignorant man and a pretender, and treated like a fool and a madman. And finally, he was insulted in his power, by being considered a sorcerer or magician who produced false miracles by means of the knowledge and power of Satan.

**160.** His disciples themselves were a cause of suffering: one of them sold out and betrayed him, their leader denied him; and all the others abandoned him. He suffered too from persons of every rank of society: kings, governors, judges, members of the royal court, soldiers, high priests, priests, clerics and lay persons, Jews and gentiles, men and women; in general, from everyone. Even his holy Mother's presence at his death added to the burden of his sufferings, for he was compelled to see her plunged into an ocean of sorrow as she stood grieving at the foot of the Cross.

**161.** Our dear Savior suffered in all the members of his body: his head was crowned with thorns, his hair and beard were plucked out, his cheeks were slapped, his face covered with spittle; his neck and arms were bound tightly with cords, his shoulders were crushed and bent with the weight of the Cross. His hands and feet were pierced with nails, and his side and his heart were opened with a lance. His whole body was torn open mercilessly by more than five thousand blows of the scourge, so that even his bones were exposed.

All his senses were invaded by this sea of sorrow: he suffered in his sight from the mocking faces of his enemies, and from the tears and grief of his friends; in his hearing, he suffered from the insults, the false testimonies, the calumnies and the horrible blasphemies that malicious tongues hurled against him; in his sense of smell, he suffered from the vile spittle that people cast at his face; in his taste, he suffered from the burning thirst in which he was given only vinegar and gall to drink; and in the sense of touch by the excess of pain inflicted by the whip, the thorns, and the nails.

**162.** His holy soul was grievously tormented by the sins of all of us, which he felt as so many outrages done to his Father, whom he loved infinitely; and by the thought that sin was the source of damnation of many souls, who in spite of his passion and death would be lost. Moreover, he had compassion not only on all humans in general, but for each one in particular, for he knew each one individually.

These interior sufferings were heightened by their long duration: which began at the moment of his conception and lasted until his death; because by the infinite light of Wisdom he saw distinctly and had always present before him all the sufferings which would come upon him.

We must not overlook the cruelest and most frightful of all his torments, which was his abandonment on the Cross, when he cried out:

*"My God, my God, why have you forsaken me?"* (Mk 15:34, Mt 27:46).

**163.** From all this, we can conclude with St. Thomas Aquinas and the Fathers of the Church, that our sweet Jesus suffered more than all the martyrs put together, including those who have suffered and who are to suffer, up until the end of the world. If then the least suffering of the Son of God is more precious and more capable of stirring our hearts than the combined suffering of all angels and humans who could possibly have offered themselves up for us, what must be our sorrow, our gratitude and our love for him, who has endured for us, freely and with immeasurable tenderness, all that a human being can possibly suffer. *"Having joy before him, he endured the cross"* (Hb 12:2). According to the Fathers of the Church, Jesus Christ, Eternal Wisdom, could have remained in his glory in heaven, infinitely distant from our sufferings; but he preferred, out of concern for us, to descend to the earth, to become human and to be crucified. After becoming human, he could have invested his body with the same joy, the same immortality, and the same heavenly glory that he now enjoys; but he did not will to do so, for he preferred to be able to suffer.

**164.** Rupert adds this thought: that at the moment of the Incarnation, the Father proposed to

His Son the choice of saving the world through delight or through affliction; by means of honors or of rejection; by riches or by poverty; through life or through death. Thus, if he had wanted to, he could have chosen joy, delight, pleasure, honors, glory and riches as the means by which to redeem humans and lead them with him to paradise. But he chose rather adversity and the Cross, so as to render to God, his Father, more glory, and to humankind the evidence of a greater love.

**165.** Further, he loved us so much, that instead of shortening his suffering, he willed to prolong it and to endure immeasurably more. This is why, on the Cross, when he was overwhelmed by insults and crushed with pain as if he had not yet suffered enough, he cried out "*I thirst.*" For what did he thirst? St. Lawrence Justinian offers an answer: "His thirst came from the ardor of his love and the flowing fountain of his abundant charity. He yearned for us and ardently desired to give himself to us.

**166.** After all these considerations, have we not good reason to exclaim with St. Francis of Paola: "O God of Love! O the excess of love that you showed us in suffering and dying for us!" or with St. Mary Magdalene of Pazzi, kissing a crucifix: "O love, how little are you known!" or with St. Francis of Assisi, trudging through the muddy streets, "Oh! Jesus, my crucified love, is not known! Jesus, my Love, is not loved!"

In the liturgy, the Church has us say every day: "The world has not known Jesus Christ, Incarnate Wisdom." For to speak truly, to know what our Lord endured for us and yet to refuse, as the world does, to love him ardently in return is something that is morally impossible.

## The Triumph of The Cross

(Canticle 19:1;102: 5-10, 12)

The cross is a mystery most
profound here below
Without abundant light it can
never be known.
Only the noble-hearted are able
to comprehend it.
Yet, understand it we must if we
are to be saved.

The way to our homeland is
the way of the cross.
It is the way of life; it is the way of kings.
Blessed cross of Calvary,
as long as it endures.

Each stone the builders use on
Holy Zion's heights
Is cut and made to fit or thrown to the devil.
Blessed cross....

What value has the triumph,
of the greatest conqueror
If he win not the glory of self-control through
crosses? Blessed cross...

Despite sense and nature, politics and reason,
The truth does assure us: The cross is a great
gift. Blessed cross...

The cross is the princess where we truly find
All grace all wisdom and divinity.
Blessed cross…

God could not resist her singular beauty;
The cross made Him come down to our human-
ity. Blessed cross…

He thought her so stunning,
He made her His honor
His eternal companion, His heart's loving
spouse. Blessed cross…

## Chapter 14

### Eternal Wisdom's Triumph through and by the Cross

167. NOW I am going to unfold for you what I think is Eternal Wisdom's greatest secret "*the secret of the king*" (Th 12:7), and that is the Cross.

Indeed, "the *thoughts of Eternal Wisdom are high above the thoughts of human beings, even the wisest of them*" (Is 55:8-9). This God of Majesty wishes to redeem the world, scatter and banish the demons, shut the doors of hell and open the gates of heaven to humanity, and render infinite glory to the Eternal Father. This is her immense and all-embracing vision, her difficult labor, her vast undertaking. What means would be chosen by Wisdom, "*who by her knowledge reaches from one end of the universe to the other, who orders all things gently and firmly*" (Ws 8:1)? Her arm is so powerful that with a simple gesture she could destroy any obstacle in order to accomplish her purpose. Yes, with a word of her mouth she can annihilate and she can create. But how can I put into words what I am trying to say? She has only to will a thing in order to bring it about.

**168.** Yet her love sets limits to her power. She wants to become flesh to prove her love to humankind. She wants to come down to earth herself in order to raise humanity to the heavens. So be it! We might then expect Incarnate Wisdom to make his appearance in glory, accompanied by armies of angels, or at least by huge crowds of chosen human beings. Unburdened by poverty, failure, humiliation, or weakness, and surrounded instead by a brilliant and impressive royal court, he would master his enemies and win all hearts by his attractions, delights, and magnificent generosity in bestowing his gifts. Surely we should expect nothing less.

Yet wonder of wonders! Eternal Wisdom's glance falls upon something that is a stumbling block and a horror to the Jews, and an object of foolishness to the gentiles. She sees a miserable block of wood that is used to condemn and to torture the most wicked and rejected of criminals. It is a scaffold, an instrument for hanging criminals, a cross. Towards this Cross she inclines her gaze; upon it she casts her favor. More than all that is magnificent in heaven and on earth, she cherishes this Cross and chooses it to be the instrument of her conquests, the ornament of her majesty, the treasure of her empire, and the friend and spouse of her heart. *"O the depth of the Wisdom and knowledge of God! How astonishing is her choice; how impossible to understand yet immensely high are her designs!"* (Rm 11:33). How unbelievable is her love for the Cross!

**169.** Wisdom Incarnate loved the Cross from her infancy. At her very entry into this world, in the womb of her mother, she accepted the Cross from the hands of her Eternal Father. She planted it in the midst of her heart so that it might rule over her life, saying "*From childhood have I loved it*" (Ws 8:2). At her very entry into this world, in the womb of her mother, she accepted the Cross from the hands of her Eternal Father. She planted it in the midst of her heart so that it might rule over her life, saying, "*My God, I will place your law in the midst of my heart*" (Ps 39:11). "God, my Father, I chose the Cross while I was still in your bosom; I chose it again in the womb of my mother. I love it with all my might, and I place it in the depth of my heart to be my spouse and my mistress."[1]

**170.** During her whole life, Wisdom energetically pursued the Cross. She was like a thirsty deer[2] running from village to village, from town to town; when she walked, it seemed with giant steps towards Calvary. She often spoke of her coming sufferings and death to her apostles and disciples, and even to the prophets who were present at her Transfiguration. She gave voice to the theme of her desire: "*With tremendous longing have I desired to eat this Passover with you*" (Lk 22:15). Thus, all her concentration and all her

1 Cf. Ws 8:2
2 Cf. Ps 41:1

journeys, all her longing and all her seeking was focused on the Cross. To die in its embrace was for her the high point of glory and the peak of fulfilment.

At her incarnation, she espoused the Cross with inexpressible love. She sought it out and carried it joyfully throughout her whole life, which was a continuous cross. Hastening to overtake it and die in its embrace on Calvary, she said: "*What constraint I am under until it is accomplished!*" (Lk12:50). "What is holding me back? Why can I not embrace it immediately, this dear Cross of Calvary?"

**171.** Finally she reached the fulfilment of her desire. Covered with blame, she was nailed at last to the Cross, and, as it were, was irrevocably united to it. She died joyfully upon it, as if in the embrace of a dear friend, on a couch of honor and triumph.

**172.** Do not imagine that in her triumph she distanced herself from the Cross, or cast it aside. Far from it! She became so identified with the Cross that no angel, nor human nor any creature of heaven or earth could ever separate her from it. Their bond is indissoluble, their union eternal.

Never the Cross without Jesus,
nor Jesus without the Cross!

By dying upon it, she rendered the shamefulness of the Cross so glorious, its poverty so enriching, its sorrows so sweet, and its rigors so attractive, that she lifted it up, as it were, to her own divine level, so that it became an object of adoration for angels and humans. She thus required all her subjects to adore it as they adore her. Although she restricts created beings, however exalted, including her own mother, from receiving adoration, this honor is allowed to be given to her cherished Cross. We know that on judgment day even the most respected relics of the saints will cease to exist. But with the Cross it is a different story. Wisdom will command the Seraphim and Cherubim to search throughout the whole world gathering its fragments which, by her gracious power, she will then reassemble into the one true Cross on which she died. At her command this Cross will be carried in triumph by the angels singing hymns of rejoicing. Preceded by her Cross on a cloud of luminous glory surpassing in brightness anything ever beheld, she will judge the world by it and with it.

How great will be the joy of the friends of the Cross at this sight! As for its enemies, they will be unable to bear its blinding light; they will beg the mountains to fall upon them and the depths of hell to swallow them up.

**173.** While waiting for this glorious Day of Judgment, Wisdom has decreed that the Cross be the insignia, the mark, and the shield of all the elect. She receives no child who is not marked with it, no disciple who does not display it openly and without shame. To anyone not willing to carry it in his heart without hesitation, and on his shoulders without dragging it, she says: "*If anyone wants to come after me, let him renounce himself, take up his cross, and follow me*" (Lk 9:23).

She accepts into her service no soldier who does not bear it as his shield of defense and his arm of attack against the enemies he must overthrow. This is her cry, "*Be confident. I have overcome the world. In this sign you will conquer*" (Jn 16:33). "Trust me, soldiers, I am your captain. By the Cross I gain victory[3] over my enemies, and by the same sign you will too."

**174.** She has hidden so many graces; so much life and joy in the Cross, that she reveals its treasures only to very special friends. She has other precious secrets that she shows to certain of her friends, to the apostles for example: "*All things I have made known to you*" (Jn 15:15). But the secrets of the Cross she reserves for those

3 In 312, victorious in his battle against Maxence, Constantine became emperor. According to legend, the day before this confrontation, Constantine saw the chrism (monogram of Christ) in the sky and heard this sentence.

who have earned them by their fidelity and by their labors. One must indeed be 'little', humble, austere, recollected, and of little account to the 'world' to know the mystery of the Cross, a mystery which remains hidden today not only to Jews, pagans, Muslims and heretics, to the wise of this world and to fallen-away Catholics, but even to the seemingly devout and the very devout. The mystery of the Cross is a stumbling block and an object of ridicule and avoidance, not just theoretically (never before has it been so much talked and written about), but in practice, because people fear it, complain about it, and excuse themselves from it. They disappear when there is something to suffer.

One day, upon seeing the Cross, Incarnate Wisdom declared in a radiant outburst of joy: "*I bless you Father, Lord of heaven and earth, for hiding these things from the learned and the clever and revealing them to little children*" (Lk 10:21).

**175.** If the knowledge of the mystery of the Cross is such a special grace, how great must be the reward and the satisfaction of attaining it! It is a gift that Eternal Wisdom pours out generously but only on her closest friends, and then only to those who have desired it, asked for it, and have been really insistent in their prayers for it. We can compare this gift to the gift of faith by which we are able to please God, commune with God, and conquer God's enemies. In fact, without faith we would be lost. Yet the Cross is a still greater gift.

According to St. John Chrysostom, Peter was happier to be in prison for Jesus Christ than to be on the mountain of Tabor with Him in His glory; he was more honored carrying chains on his feet than with the keys of paradise in his hands. Paul esteemed it a greater glory to be put into chains for his Savior than to be carried up to the third heaven. God bestowed a greater favor on the apostles and martyrs in giving them His Cross to carry in their humiliations, privations, and torments than in granting the gift of miracles or of converting the world.

All those to whom Eternal Wisdom gave herself have desired the Cross, sought after it, and welcomed it. Whenever they had occasion to suffer, they cried out from the bottom of their hearts with St. Andrew: "O dear Cross, so long desired."

**176.** The Cross is worthy of our love for many reasons:

1. Because by it we come to resemble Jesus Christ.
2. Because it makes us worthy children of the Eternal Father, worthy members

of Jesus Christ, and worthy temples of the Holy Spirit. God the Father "chastises all the children whom he accepts" (Hb 12:6). Jesus Christ accepts as His own only those who carry their crosses. The Holy Spirit dresses and polishes all the living stones of the heavenly Jerusalem *i.e.*, the chosen ones.

3. The Cross is precious because it enlightens the spirit and imparts to it more knowledge than all the books in the world could ever do. "The one who has not been tried, what does he know?" (Si 34:9).

4. When it is carried well, it is the source, the nourishment, and the proof of love. The Cross sets alight the fire of divine love in the heart by detaching it from creatures. It feeds and intensifies this love; just as wood is food for the fire, so the Cross is the food of love. And it is the most reliable proof of our love for God. This is the evidence that God gave to show His love for us; and it is also the evidence that God asks as proof of our love for Him.

5. The Cross is precious because it is an abundant source of every delight and

consolation, and it produces joy, peace, and grace in the soul.

6. Finally, it is precious because for the one who bears it, it works "an immense weight of glory in heaven" (2 Cor 4:17).

**177.** If we understood the value of the Cross like St. Peter of Alcantara, we would have novenas made to obtain this rare and delightful foretaste of paradise. Like St. Theresa, we would say: "Either to suffer or to die." Or with St. Mary Magdalene of Pazzi, we would pray: "Not to die but to suffer." Like St. John of the Cross we would ask only for the grace to suffer and to be despised for his sake. As he said to a holy person after his death: "In heaven the only earthly thing that is valued is the Cross." And our Lord said to one of his servants, "I have crosses of such great value that there is nothing greater that my Mother, powerful as she is, can obtain from me for her faithful servants."

**178.** You who believe yourselves to be wise and good people according to the standards of the world, you will not understand this mysterious language of the Cross. You are too attached to your small pleasures; you are too taken up with ensuring your own comfort; you are too afraid of being scorned or humiliated; in short, you are too opposed to the Cross of Jesus. You may esteem and even praise the Cross in general, but not when it comes to your own cross. This you avoid as much as you can, or else you drag it along reluctantly, complaining and losing your patience. You act like the oxen who bore the Ark of the Covenant: bellowing and protesting while pulling their load, unaware that it contained what is most precious in the world.[4]

**179.** The number of fools and unhappy people is boundless says Wisdom, because countless numbers of people do not know the value of the Cross and, therefore, carry it reluctantly.

But you, true disciples of Eternal Wisdom, if you have trials and afflictions, if you suffer persecution for justice's sake, if you are treated like the rubbish of this world, take comfort, "*rejoice, and be glad*" (Mt 5:12). The cross that you carry is a precious gift which the blessed in heaven envy you, for the gift of the Cross is now outside their experience. All there is of honor, glory and virtue in God and in his Holy Spirit is yours, "*for your reward is great in heaven*" (Mt 5:12), and even on earth, because of the spiritual graces it obtains for you.

**180.** Friends of Jesus Christ, drink of his bitter chalice, and you will draw closer and closer to him. Suffer with him and you will be glorified with him. Suffer patiently and even joyfully just

4 Cf. Is 6:12

a little while longer, and this momentary pain will be followed by an eternity of happiness!

Ever since Incarnate Wisdom entered heaven by way of the Cross, it is necessary to enter after her by the same way. *The Imitation of Christ* instructs us that no matter which way we turn, we will always find crosses. Ours will be the cross of the faithful ones if we take it up patiently and cheerfully for the love of God; but it will be the cross of the lost ones, if we bear it reluctantly and impatiently. Those who belong to the last-named group will be doubly miserable because they will be forced to continue their complaint in hell: "In the world we have toiled and suffered, and now here we are among the damned."

True Wisdom is not to be found on earth or in the hearts of those who live for their comfort. For she is so at home with the Cross that, you will never find her elsewhere in this world. She is so identified with the Cross that one can truly say:

Wisdom is the Cross and the Cross is Wisdom.

## Power of Patience

(Canticle 11:8, 13, 7)

The cross has abundant power,
It is the spur of virtue,
It is the brace and hope
Of the poor despondent sinner.
This cross is heavy, it is true,
Yet when we love its holy weight,
The soul abroad is most at ease
And both laugh and weep.

"Will anyone come to live with me?"
Asked Jesus Christ quite clearly;
"Will any follow where I will go?"
Take up your cross and carry it.
With my cross I walk ahead,
I want your suffering like mine,
Without complaint
Or stopping to look back.

It is you, dear cross that rule
Over all the enemies of God.
Yet in this lowly place no one knows
That your victory is divine.
The world deems you ugly
Flesh is fearful of your strictness.
The devil looks at you with hate,
While your greatness I adore.

## Chapter 15

### Two Means to Obtain Divine Wisdom

### The First Means: An Ardent Desire

**181.** "*HOW long, O children of humankind, will you continue looking earthwards with a heavy heart? How long will you go after vanity and set your sights on illusion?*" (Ps 4:3). Why don't you turn your eyes and your hearts towards Wisdom, who, of all the possible things that one could desire, is the most desirable? For to make herself attractive to humans, Wisdom reveals her origin, unveils her beauty, displays her treasures, and gives a thousand proofs of the desire She has for you to desire and seek after her. *"Desire, therefore, to hear my words"* (Ws 6:12). "*She goes forth to meet those who desire her*" (Ws 6:14). *"The desire of Wisdom leads to a kingdom which is eternal"* (Ws 6:21).

**182.** The desire for Wisdom is itself a great gift of God given as a reward for the faithful observance of God's commandments.

> *My child, if you desire Wisdom, keep the commandments, and the Lord will bestow it on you. Reflect on the instructions of the Lord, busy yourself at all times with His commandments and He Himself will give you a heart, and the desire of Wisdom will be given to you* (Ws 1:33; 6:17).

*Wisdom will never enter the soul of a wrong-doer, nor dwell in a body enslaved to sin* (Ws 1:4).

This desire for Wisdom must be sincere and holy, accompanied by a faithful observance of God's commandments; for "*there are a million thoughtless*" (Qo 1:15) and undisciplined people who desire Wisdom or, more accurately, they wish for Wisdom; but it is a vain and even destructive desire if it does not lead them to abandon sin and make the necessary sacrifices.

*All day long the godless one is tortured by desire* (Pr 21:25). *For the Holy Spirit of instruction flees deceitfulness, is dismayed by lack of comprehension, and is driven away from the soul by the onset of vice* (Ws 1:5).

**183.** Solomon, who is the model that the Holy Spirit gave us for obtaining Wisdom, did not receive this gift without having long desired it, sought for it, and prayed for it.

*"I prayed and understanding was given to me, I pleaded urgently and the spirit of Wisdom came to me* (Ws 7:7). *Wisdom I loved and searched for from my youth. I resolved to have her as my bride. I went every which way, seeking how to get her"* (Ws 8:2, 18).

To obtain this great treasure of Wisdom, one must be a 'person of desire,' like Solomon and Daniel.

### The Second Means: Continuous Prayer

**184.** The greater the gift of God, the more difficulty one experiences in obtaining it. So we can imagine what prayer and what effort is required to obtain the gift of Wisdom, which is the greatest of all God's gifts.

Let us listen to Wisdom speaking in her own voice: "*Seek and you shall find, knock and it shall be opened to you, ask and it shall be given to you*" (Mt 7:7; Lk 11:9). It is as if she said, "If you want to find me, seek me; if you want to enter my palace, you must knock at my door; if you wish to receive me, you must ask for me." No one finds me without searching for me; no one enters my house without knocking at my door; no one comes to possess me without asking for me. It is prayer that accomplishes everything."

Prayer is the ordinary channel through which God communicates His grace, and especially His Wisdom. The world had been praying four thousand years for the incarnation of Divine Wisdom. For fourteen years Mary prepared herself by prayer to receive Him in her womb. Solomon received Wisdom only after praying ardently for her for a long time:

> *I went to the Lord and besought him, and I said with all my heart:*
>
> *Grant me this Wisdom who is seated beside you on your throne!* (Ws 8:21; 9:4).
>
> *If any of you lacks Wisdom, let him ask God, and it shall be given him, for God gives his gifts to all abundantly and ungrudgingly.* (Jm 1:5).

Note that the Holy Spirit does not say, "If anyone lacks charity, humility, patience, etc." although these are most excellent virtues, but rather, "If anyone lacks Wisdom." For in asking for Wisdom we ask for all the virtues that she contains.

**185.** To attain her, "*one must, therefore, ask*" (Jm 1:5). But the question is, how?

The first quality is a lively and unwavering faith. "*We should pray for this gift with a lively, unhesitating faith. The one who wavers in faith, should not expect to receive anything from the Lord*" (Jm 1:6-7).

**186.** Secondly, we must pray for it with a pure faith, not counting on feelings of consolation, visions, or special revelations. Although such things may be good and true as they have been in the case of some saints, it is always dangerous to rely on them. For the more our faith is dependent on extraordinary graces and feelings of consolation, the less pure and worthy of reward it really is. The Holy Spirit has revealed to us the greatness and the beauty of Wisdom; He has also revealed the desire that God has to bestow this gift upon us and our own need of it as well. These are strong enough motives to make us desire and beg God ardently for Wisdom with fiery perseverance and the most persistent faith.

**187.** Simple faith is both the cause and the effect of Wisdom in our soul. The more faith we have, the more wisdom we possess. And the opposite is also true: the more wisdom, the greater our faith. "The just person lives by faith:"[1] without seeing, without feeling, without tasting, and without faltering. "God has said it or has promised it." This is the foundation stone of all the prayers and all the actions of the wise ones. On this they stand, even when it seems to them from a human point of view that God is blind to their desperate situation, deaf to their prayers, powerless before their enemies, empty-handed in the face of their need. On faith's foundation they remain even though indeed they may be troubled by distractions and doubts, or assaulted by darkness in the mind, illusions in the imagination, weariness and boredom in the heart, or by anguish or sadness in their souls.

1 Cf. Rm 1:17

People who are truly wise do not ask to see extraordinary things, such as saints have seen, nor to experience sweet emotions in their prayers. They ask *"with faith"* (Jm 1:6) for divine Wisdom. And they feel surer that Wisdom *"will be given them"* (Jm 1:5) than if it were sworn for by an angel come down from heaven. They believe only because God has said it: *"All who pray in the proper manner will receive what they ask for* (Lk 11:10). *"If you then, being evil, know how to give good things to your children, how much more will your heavenly Father give the good spirit* of Wisdom *to those who ask him?"* (Lk 11:13).

**188.** Thirdly, we must ask for Wisdom with perseverance. To obtain this precious pearl which is an infinite treasure, we must approach God with holy insistence. Without such steadfast petitioning we shall never attain it. It is not like some ordinary grace such as those that people commonly pray for. Often when they have prayed for some time perhaps years and do not see God's answer to their prayers, they get discouraged and give up praying, believing that God does not want to listen to them; thus they lose the fruit of their prayers and offend God, whose pleasure is to give, and who always hears our prayers one way or the other if they are well said.

So those who want to obtain Wisdom let them demand it day and night, without allowing themselves to grow weary or frustrated. A thousand times happy will that person be who obtains this gift after ten, twenty, or thirty years of prayer, or even just before death. And if they receive it after having spent a whole lifetime seeking and asking, and accumulating the merit of their labors and crosses, let them be aware that it is not due to them in strict justice, nor even as a reward, but is given out of sheer mercy as a totally free gift.

**189.** For Wisdom will not come to negligent souls who are inconstant in their prayers and half-hearted in their seeking. She will come instead to those who are like that man in the gospel who went in the night to knock on the door of a friend to ask him for three loaves of bread. Notice carefully that it is Wisdom herself in this parable who tells us the way we ought to ask in order to obtain what we ask for. This friend knocks and redoubles his insistence, four or five times, each time louder and more assertively, even though the hour is near midnight, even though his friend is in bed, and even though he has already been refused and sent away several times like a selfish nuisance. Finally, the friend who was in bed, finding himself so pressured by the demands of his friend at the door, gets up, opens the door and gives him what he wants.[2]

2 Cf. Lk 11:5-8

**190.** This is the way we must pray to obtain Wisdom; and without fail, sooner or later, God, who actually wants to be disturbed by our insistent prayer, will get up and open the door of His mercy, and give us the three loaves of Wisdom: the bread of life, the bread of understanding, and the bread of angels.

The following are some prayers formulated by the Holy Spirit to ask for Wisdom.

### Prayer of Solomon to Obtain Divine Wisdom

**191.** *O God of my fathers and Lord of mercy, you made the world by your word, and you fashioned human beings by your Wisdom to exercise dominion over all the creatures you have made, to govern the world in fairness and justice, and to give judgment with a clear heart. Give me this Wisdom who sits with you on your throne.*

*Do not reject me from the number of your children, for I am your servant and the son of your handmaid, a weak man with little time to live and with a poor understanding of justice and law. For even though a person be considered perfect in human terms, such a one is of no value if your Wisdom does not dwell in him.*[3]

3 Montfort purposely omits verses 7 and 8, which are specifically related to the historic mission of Solomon to reign over his people and build a temple in Jerusalem. With this omission, the prayer then retains a universal scope.

**192.** *It is your Wisdom who designed all your works, who was with you when you made the world; who knows what is pleasing in your sight, and what is essentially right in your commandments.*

*Send her then from your sanctuary in heaven and from the throne of your majesty, so that she may be with me and work with me; so that I may know what is pleasing to you; for she possesses knowledge and insight into everything. She will guide me rightly in everything I do and protect me by her power. My actions will then be pleasing to you, and I will lead Your people with justice, and be worthy of the throne of my Father. For what human being can know the intentions of God or perceive the divine will with accuracy? Human ideas lack boldness, and our plans are tentative; for a body that will eventually die and decay weighs heavily upon one's soul, and an earthly dwelling burdens a spirit distracted by many cares. It is hard for us to understand what is happening upon earth; in fact it is very difficult for us to figure out the meaning of what is happening right in front of our eyes. How then can we comprehend what is happening in heaven?*

*How can we know your thoughts unless you give us your Wisdom and send us your*

*Holy Spirit from on high, to direct the paths of us who live upon the earth and teach us how to be pleasing to you? O Lord, since the beginning of time it is through your Wisdom that all those who have been pleasing to you have been saved* (Ws 9:1-6, 9-19).

193. To vocal prayer we must add mental prayer, which gives light to the mind and fire to the heart, and also disposes the soul to listen to the voice of Wisdom, savoring her delights and enjoying her treasures.

For my part, I know of no more effective way of drawing down the reign of God, Eternal Wisdom dwelling within us, than to combine vocal and mental prayer in reciting the holy rosary while meditating on the fifteen mysteries.

## The Desire for Wisdom

(Canticle 124:1-5)

O Wisdom come, a poor soul begs you
By the blood of my gentle Jesus,
By Mary's womb
We shall not be disappointed. (*Twice*)

Why do you so prolong my martyrdom?
I seek you night and day!
Come, my soul longs for you,
Come, I am languishing of love. (*Twice*)

My beloved, open, I knock at your door,
Ah! It is no stranger,
It is a heart, by love transported
Who has no dwelling place but you! (*Twice*)

If you do not want me to be yours,
Then let me pester you.
Leave me always in the anguish
Of seeking and never finding you. (*Twice*)

I cast myself in spirit at your throne
If you want nothing to do with me,
At least give me some alms
For the faith-filled poor. (*Twice*)

# Chapter 16

## The Third Means to Obtain Wisdom

### Universal Mortification

194. *WISDOM is not found among those who live comfortably.*[1] It is the Holy Spirit who tells us that Wisdom is not found among those who indulge their passions and appetites. *"Those who walk the way of the flesh cannot please God"* (Rm 8:8), *"for the wisdom of the flesh is at enmity with God"* (Rm 8:7). *"My spirit does not dwell in people, because they are flesh"* (Gn 6:3).

Those who belong to Jesus Christ, Wisdom Incarnate, *"have crucified their flesh with its strong desires and addictive tendencies"* (Gn 5:24); they always bear in their bodies the mortification of Jesus and they discipline themselves continuously; *"they bear their cross every day"* (Lk 9:23), for they have "buried themselves with Christ Jesus."[2]

These words of the Holy Spirit make it as clear as day that to possess Wisdom Incarnate, Jesus Christ, one must practice mortification, renunciation of the world, and renunciation of oneself.

1 Cf. Jb 28:13

2 Cf. 2 Cor 4:10; Rm 6:4

**195.** Do not imagine that Wisdom, who is purer than the rays of the sun, enters a soul and body that are soiled by the pleasures of the senses. Do not think that she gives her repose, her incomparable peace, to those who enjoy the distractions of the world and the companionship of the worldly. "*To those who are victorious* over the world and themselves *I give my hidden manna.*"[3]

This lovely sovereign, who by her infinite light knows and distinguishes every separate thing in a moment, nevertheless "*seeks persons worthy of her*" (Ws 6:17). She seeks them because their number is so small. She finds scarcely anyone sufficiently detached, sufficiently interior, and sufficiently mortified to be worthy of her person, her treasures, and her offer of union.

**196.** Thus, as the condition for communicating herself, she does not ask for just a partial mortification that lasts only a few days, but a mortification that is universal and continuous, courageous and discreet.

Such mortification has the following six qualities.

**197.** 1) One can become detached by leaving behind the goods of this world as did the apostles, the disciples, the first Christians, and the

3 Cf. Ac 2:17

consecrated religious of today. It is the quickest and easiest, the surest way, to come to the possession of Wisdom. Or at least one must detach the heart from material goods, possessing them as if one did not possess them; without eagerness to acquire them, without concern for preserving them; and without distress and frustration when they are taken away. This is actually a very difficult thing to achieve.

**198.** 2) One must avoid conforming to the trends and fashions of the world: in clothes, houses, furnishings, food, entertainment, and all the other areas that have to do with image and lifestyle. *"Do not model your behavior on the expectations of the world"* (Rm 12:2). It is more important to practice this than you might think.

**199.** 3) One must not believe or follow the false principles of the world; one must not think, speak, or act in imitation of worldly people. Their ideas are as contrary to the idea of Wisdom as darkness is to light, or death to life. Examine carefully their attitudes and words, for they think and speak badly about all the great truths. While it is true they do not tell outright falsehoods, in fact they disguise their lies under an appearance of truth. Although they do not believe they are lying, nevertheless they do. If they do not openly recommend sin, they promote it as if it were virtue or an aspect of one's 'honor'; or else they dismiss it as something small and of no account. This is how the world has learned from the devil to disguise the ugliness of sin and falsehood. This is the bad faith that St. John spoke of: "*The whole world is in the power of the evil one*" (1Jn 5:19) and now more than ever.

**200.** 4) As much as possible, we must abstain from useless socializing, not only when it presents a clear danger to us, but whenever it is a waste of time, even if the persons whose company we seek seem devout. One who wishes to become wise and completely whole must practice the three golden counsels that Wisdom gave to St. Arsenius: "Flee, hide, and be silent. As the great saints[4] did, avoid human company as much as you can." "*Let your life be hidden with Christ in God*" (Col 3:3). Finally, be silent with others in order to converse with Wisdom. "*The person who keeps silent is considered wise*" (Ws 20:5).

**201.** 5) To obtain Wisdom we have to mortify the body. This we do not only by submitting patiently to sickness, various bodily ailments, the discomforts of the weather, and even the sufferings that others impose on us, but also by voluntarily inflicting some mortifications on

4 *The Imitation of Christ*

ourselves. These might be fasts, vigils, or other austerities such as the saints performed.

To do this takes courage, because the flesh quite naturally makes an idol of itself. Moreover, the world despises and rejects as useless any mortification of the body. It is extraordinary how ingenious people can be when it is a question of dispensing themselves from the austerities of the saints. Of each of them it can be said to some extent: He has brought his body into subjection by vigils, fasts, and disciplines, by enduring cold and nakedness and every kind of penance; and he has made a solemn pact with his own body not to give it any rest in this world. The Holy Spirit has said of the saints: "*They were enemies of the stained robe of the flesh*" (Jude 23).

**202.** 6) In order to ensure that these exterior, voluntary mortifications achieve what they are meant to, it is necessary to join them to mortification of the judgment and will by practicing holy obedience; because, without obedience, all mortification is tainted with self-will, and is often more pleasing to the devil than to God.

This is why we should not attempt any significant mortification without taking counsel. "*I, Wisdom, live in the same household as counsel*" (Pr 8:12). "*Whoever trusts in his own judgment is a fool*" (Pr 28:26). "*The wise one does everything with counsel"* (Pr 13:17). The important advice that the Holy Spirit gives us is this: "*Never act without counsel, and you will not regret your actions. Always ask advice of a wise person"* (Tb 4:19).

By obedience, we eliminate self-love, which spoils everything. By obedience the smallest action becomes meritorious. In this way we find protection from the illusions of the devil; we gain victory over our enemies; and "we arrive safely, almost while sleeping, in the harbor of salvation."[5]

All that I have said is included in the one great counsel: "Leave all and you will find all"[6] in finding Jesus Christ Wisdom Incarnate.

5 St. John Chrysostom
6 *The Imitation of Christ*

# Chapter 17

## The Fourth Means to Obtain Divine Wisdom

### True Devotion to the Blessed Virgin Mary

**203.** THE greatest of all means and the most wonderful of all secrets for obtaining and conserving divine Wisdom is this: a loving and true devotion to the Blessed Virgin.

Mary alone found grace before God for herself and for the whole human family. She alone attracted Eternal Wisdom to become incarnate, and she alone brought Incarnate Wisdom into the world. Thus, one could say that only she, through the action of the Holy Spirit, has the power to incarnate him in predestinate souls.

The patriarchs, the prophets and the saints of the Old Testament yearned, implored, and begged God for the incarnation of Eternal Wisdom, but none of them was able to merit it. Only Mary, by her awe-inspiring virtue, was able to reach the throne of God and merit this infinite blessing. She it was who became the Mother, the Mistress, and the Throne of Divine Wisdom.

**204.** She is Wisdom's most worthy Mother, because she incarnated her in the world as the fruit of her womb: "*Blessed is the fruit of your womb*" (Lk 1:42) Jesus. So wherever Jesus is, in heaven or on earth, in our tabernacles or in our hearts, it can truly be said that he remains in a fundamental relationship to Mary: she alone is the tree of life, and he is its sole fruit. It follows that whoever wants to have this admirable fruit in their heart must have the tree which produced it: whoever wants to have Jesus must have Mary.

**205.** In a certain way, we can say that Mary is also the Mistress of Divine Wisdom not that she is above Divine Wisdom, who is true God, or that she is the equal of Wisdom, it would be blasphemous to believe that or to teach it, but because God the Son, Eternal Wisdom, submitted himself perfectly to her as to his mother. In so acting, he gave her for all eternity a kind of natural maternal power over him which to us seems beyond comprehension, not just for the duration of his earthly life, but even in heaven for not only does glory not destroy nature, but indeed it perfects nature.

Thus Jesus remains the child of Mary as much as ever in heaven, and Mary in turn remains the mother of Jesus. In this capacity, she retains a certain power over him, and he submits to her in a certain way, because he wills it. Thus Mary, by her powerful prayers and divine maternity, obtains whatever she wants from Jesus; she gives him to whomever she wishes; and she brings him forth every day in souls, as she wishes.

**206.** How happy is the soul who has won the good graces of Mary! Such a soul must count itself assured of possessing Wisdom in good time; for since Mary loves those who love her, she communicates to them her blessings with a generous hand, even the infinite blessing which includes all others, Jesus the fruit of her womb.

**207.** If it is true to say that Mary is, in some sense the Mistress of Incarnate Wisdom, what is there left to say about the power she has over all the graces and gifts of God, and of the freedom she enjoys to distribute them as she sees fit?

She is, say the holy Fathers, the immense ocean of all the splendors of God, the great storehouse of all his gifts: She is both his inexhaustible treasure, and the treasurer and dispenser of all his graces.

Having given His Son to her, God wills that we should receive all things by her hand; indeed He allows no heavenly gift to descend to earth unless it passes through her as a channel.

*"It is of her fullness that we have all received"* (Jn 1:16). Thus, if there is in us any grace, any hope of salvation, it is a gift coming to us from God through Mary. She is so much Mistress of God's gifts that she gives them to whom she wills, as much as she wishes, when she wishes, and in the way she wishes. These gifts include

all the graces of God, all the virtues of Jesus Christ, and all the gifts of the Holy Spirit, indeed all the graces of nature, grace and glory.

These are the thoughts and expressions of the holy Fathers. I do not take the time to cite all the Latin texts here. But be assured that whatever gifts this sovereign and lovely Princess gives to us, she will not be content until she gives us the gift of Incarnate Wisdom, Jesus her Son. She is active every day, looking for souls worthy of Wisdom so that she can pour out this gift upon them.

**208.** Moreover, Mary is the royal throne of Eternal Wisdom. In Mary she manifests her grandeurs and displays her treasures; in her she takes her delight. There is no place in heaven or on earth where Eternal Wisdom reveals so much magnificence and takes so much pleasure as in the incomparable Mary.

This is why the holy Fathers call her the Sanctuary of the Divinity, the Delightful Resting Place of the Holy Trinity, the Throne of God, the City of God, the Altar of God, the Temple of God, the World of God, and the Paradise of God. All these titles and praises are true, with respect to the different marvels that the Most High has worked in Mary.

**209.** So it is through Mary alone that we can obtain Wisdom.

But if we were given a gift as great as Wisdom, where would we lodge her? What house, what seat, or what throne would we offer to this princess so pure and so brilliant that the rays of the sun are no more than gloomy darkness and mud in her presence? Perhaps you will say that it is only our heart that she asks for, that our heart is the gift we must give her, and the lodging we should offer her.

**210.** But do we not know that our heart is stained with impurities, made from the flesh of the earth and full of passions, and therefore unworthy to receive so noble and holy a guest? And besides that, even though we might have ten thousand hearts like our own to offer her as a throne, she would still be right to decline our offer, turn away from our persistence, and even accuse us of boldness and presumption for proposing to lodge her in such an unhealthy and unsuitable place?

**211.** So what should we do then to make our heart worthy of her? Here I give you a wonderful piece of advice, a truly precious secret: Let us, in a manner of speaking, invite Mary into our house by consecrating ourselves to her without reserve as her servants and slaves. In her honor and into her hands, let us empty ourselves of all that is dearest to us, keeping back nothing; and this good Mistress, who has never allowed herself to be outdone in generosity will give herself to us in an incomprehensible but real way. Eternal Wisdom will then come to dwell in us, as on a most glorious throne.

**212.** Mary is a holy magnet who attracts Eternal Wisdom so powerfully that she cannot resist coming to her. Like a magnet, Mary attracts Wisdom to earth for the sake of all humans, and continues to attract her every day to each particular place where she resides. Once we have Mary dwelling with us, we can easily and in a short time through her intercession have Wisdom. Of all the ways to have Jesus Christ, Mary is the most certain, the easiest, the shortest, and the holiest.

Even if we should perform the most extreme penances, undertake the most arduous pilgrimages and the greatest labors, even if we should shed our blood for the acquisition of Wisdom, if devotion to the Blessed Virgin is not in all these efforts, they would be practically useless and incapable of winning what we hope to obtain. But if Mary were to say a word on our behalf, if her love dwells with us, if we are marked with the mark of her faithful servants who keep her ways, we will obtain Divine Wisdom soon, and at little cost.

**213.** Notice that not only is Mary the Mother of Jesus, who is the head of the body of the elect[1],

1 Cf. Ep 1:22; Col 1:18.

but she is also Mother of all the members; so that it is she who conceives them, carries them in her womb, and brings them forth into the world of glory, by the grace of God which she communicates to them. This is the doctrine of the holy Fathers, among others of St. Augustine, who says that the elect are in the womb of Mary, and that she births them only at the moment when they enter into glory. Moreover, it is Mary whom God has destined "*to dwell in Jacob, to make her heritage in Israel, and to put down her roots in the chosen people*" (Si 24:13).

**214.** From these truths we must conclude:

1. In vain do we pride ourselves on being children of God and disciples of wisdom if we are not children of Mary;

2. To be counted among those who are saved, it is necessary that, by our tender and sincere devotion to her, Mary should dwell in us and take root in us;

3. It is her mission to give birth to Jesus Christ in us and to transform us into Jesus Christ, unto the perfection and *the plenitude of His age* (Eph 4:13). For Mary can say with more conviction than St. Paul said of himself, "*I give birth to you every day, my dear children,*

*until Jesus Christ* my Son, *be perfectly formed in you"* (Gal 4:19).

**215.** If anyone seeking to be devoted to the Blessed Virgin should ask me what true devotion really is, I would say in summary, that it is composed of these elements: a great esteem for her majesty, a great gratitude for her blessings, a great zeal for her glory, a continuous petitioning for her help, a total dependence on her authority, and a firm reliance on her, as well as a tender confidence in her maternal goodness.

**216.** It is also necessary to beware of false devotion to the Blessed Virgin, for the devil uses it to deceive and ensnare many souls. I won't take time to describe these false devotions; it's enough to say that True Devotion to Mary is always:

1. interior, without hypocrisy or superstition;

2. tender, without scruple and also without lukewarmness;

3. constant, without wavering or infidelity;

4. holy, without presumption or self-will.

**217.** These are some false devotions to avoid:

- Avoid being among those false and hypocritical devotees who wear their devotion externally, on their lips and their bodies only.

- Likewise avoid being among those critical and scrupulous ones who are afraid of giving too much honor to the Blessed Virgin, as though they dishonor the Son in honoring the Mother.

- Do not be one of those lukewarm devotees who serve her for selfish ends, who have neither a tender love nor a filial confidence in her, and who only have recourse to her for the acquisition or conservation of their earthly goods.

- And do not be one of those inconstant devotees who are only devoted when they are in the mood for it, and then only for a short time. These devotees withdraw from her service in times of temptation.

- Finally, do not be among the presumptuous devotees who under the cloak of a few exterior devotions, hide a heart corrupted by sin; who imagine that because of their devotions to the Blessed Virgin, they will not die without confession, and that they will be saved in spite of the sins they commit.

**218.** It is a good idea, too, to enroll in a confraternity dedicated to the Blessed Virgin, like the Confraternity of the Holy Rosary, so that you will have a structure for performing your practices.

**219.** But the most perfect and useful of all the devotions to the Blessed Virgin is to consecrate yourself entirely to her and to Jesus through her, in the manner of a slave, giving over to her by a total and everlasting consecration: your body and your soul, your possessions, both internal and external, and the value of your good actions, along with the right of disposing of them, and of all the goods you have received in the past, or that you own now, or will own in the future.

Since there are a number of books which treat of this devotion, it suffices to assure you that I have never found a more solid practice of devotion to the Virgin Mary since it is based on the example of Jesus Christ, nor one that gives more glory to God. None is more salutary to the soul, or more powerful against the enemies of salvation. Finally, there is none that is sweeter and easier.

**220.** When well practiced this devotion not only attracts Jesus Christ into the soul, but beyond that, keeps him there, and maintains him until death. For I ask you, what use would it be to go after a thousand secrets and to make a thousand efforts to obtain the treasure of Wisdom, if after receiving it, we were to have the misfortune of losing it by our infidelity as did Solomon?[2] He was wiser than we will probably ever be, stronger, and more enlightened to start with; yet he took a wrong turn and was overcome. He fell into sin and reckless folly, leaving his descendants perplexed by the paradox of his light dimmed by his darkness, as well as by his wisdom diminished by the foolishness of his sins. We could say that while his example and his writings have certainly inspired a great number of his descendants to desire and seek Wisdom, Solomon's real fall, or at least the well-founded presumption that we have of it, has also prevented countless souls from dedicating themselves to the pursuit of a goal that for all its attractiveness, seems so easily lost.

**221.** So to be in some way wiser than Solomon, it is necessary to entrust to Mary all that we possess, including the treasure of treasures, Jesus Christ, so that she can keep Him for us. We ourselves are vessels too fragile to hold this heavenly manna and precious treasure. We have at hand so many enemies who are very clever and experienced. Let us not put our faith

2 Indeed, the Bible evokes the "madness" of Solomon, consisting above all in having erected places of worship to the pagan gods that his wives worshiped (1 Ki 11:1-11; Si 47:19-20).

in our own prudence and strength. With all the disastrous experience we have of our own changeable nature and our inbuilt inconstancy, let us be wary of counting on our personal dedication and our wisdom.

**222.** Mary is wise: Let us entrust everything to her; she will know what to do with us and with what is ours, for the greater glory of God.

Mary is loving: she loves us as her children and her disciples. Let us offer her everything—we have nothing to lose, she will turn it all to our benefit.

Mary is generous: she will repay us far more than we give her; let us give what we possess, without any reserve; we will receive back a hundredfold—as they say, for a hundred little eggs, a great ox.

Mary is powerful: nothing can rob her of what we place in her safe-keeping; so let us put ourselves into her hands; and she will defend us and give us victory over all our enemies.

Mary is faithful: she does not allow anything we give her to go astray or get lost. She is the faithful Virgin par excellence, faithful both to God and to humans. She has guarded and kept faithfully all that God has entrusted to her without losing the smallest particle of it, and still, each day and with special care, she watches over all those who are under her protection and her guidance.

Let us then confide everything to her fidelity; let us attach ourselves to her as to a pillar that cannot be broken down, or an anchor that cannot be lifted or better still, Mount Sion that cannot be shaken. Thus, however blind, weak, and inconstant we are by nature, however numerous and full of evil intentions are our enemies, we will not mistake our way, we will never get lost, nor will we ever have the misfortune to lose the grace of God and the infinite treasure of Eternal Wisdom.

## New Canticle in Honor of Our Lady of Shadows

(Canticle 155:1-2, 4, 6, 15)

It is through Mary that heaven allures us.
To be happy we must love her.
Everything invites us to love her in this life.
How lovely, in her shadow let us hide.

Under her wings in the shade of her mercy
Sinners are safe.
Even the most hostile become most faithful.
How lovely, in her shadow let us hide.

May all admire the radiance of her holiness
Under the shade of her humility.
Who can fathom the mystery of her reign?
How lovely, in her shadow let us hide.

Her shining faith in its obscure splendor
Surpasses the starry sky.
All heaven sings, even her shadow is powerful.
How lovely, in her shadow let us hide.

Divine Mother reign within me,
In the shadow of your faith.
So I may believe and do the will of my Father.
How lovely, in her shadow let us hide.

## The Consecration to Jesus Christ, Incarnate Wisdom, through the Hands of Mary

**223.** Lord Jesus Christ, Son of the Father and Son of Mary,

Wisdom Eternal and Wisdom Incarnate, I adore you.

I praise you in the embrace of your Father and in the womb of Mary.

I thank you for having become human like us in order to save us.

I adore you in your Incarnation, because you freely chose to be dependent on Mary, your Mother and mine. With her and through her I long to know you more deeply and to love you more intimately. But I confess that I have sinned; I have not kept the vows of my Baptism. I know all too well my own weakness and my unfaithfulness. And so I turn to Mary so that she may satisfy to the full my desire for Divine Wisdom. I trust that she may obtain for me the grace to live out in spirit and in truth the obligations of my Baptism.

**224.** I turn, then to you, O Mary, Immaculate One. You are the Living Tabernacle of God, and the Seat of Wisdom. You are the Queen of Heaven and Earth, and the unfailing Refuge of

Sinners. Graciously accept my promises and the offering which I now make of myself.

225. Today I (*name*)…

renew with my hand in yours the promises of my Baptism.

I pledge myself with your help to struggle against evil.

I give myself completely to Jesus, Incarnate Wisdom,

So as to be more faithful to Him from now on by carrying my cross after Him all the days of my life.

226. And so, I choose you today, O Mary, to be both my Mother and my Queen. I place myself entirely in your hands with all that I am and all that I have. I give you whatever I may do in the future and whatever worth my life may have, so that you may use it for the service of the Kingdom of God.

227. O most kind-hearted of all Virgins, accept this offering of myself. Teach me not to hold back from being led by you. Grant that I may become a true disciple of your Son. Virgin most faithful, share your faithfulness with me, so that I may attain one day to "*the fullness of*

*life"* (Eph 4:13) in Jesus Christ here on earth and for all eternity. Amen.

*"Let the one who is able to understand this, understand it"* (Mt 19:12).

*"Who is wise enough to understand these marvels?"* (Ho 14:10).

## Devout Slave of Jesus in Mary

(Canticle 77:1-2, 4-5, 7-8)

Sing out my soul! Make known
To the glory of my Savior,
Mary's great mercy
Toward her poor servant.

Would that I had a voice of thunder
To proclaim far and near;
The happiest people on this earth
Are those who serve her best.

Mary is my greatest fortune
And my all at Jesus' throne.
She is my tenderness and my honor,
The treasure house of all my worth.

She is my Covenant Ark
Where all holiness I find.
She is my robe of innocence
Concealing all I lack.

She is my city of refuge
Where I cannot be harmed.
She is my ark in deluge;
There I shall never drown.

On her I am totally dependent,
On my Savior more so to depend,
Leaving everything to her care,
My body, soul and all my joy.

# Reading Guide

## Presentation

THIS reading guide does not pretend to be an in-depth commentary on *The Love of Eternal Wisdom*. It was written to help those reading it for the first time or returning to it after a while. It can be used in groups or individually.

Montfort's goal in writing this book is not to explain a doctrine or dogmas to us, but to make us meet someone who seduced and fulfilled him: Jesus Christ. But for him, Christ is more than the historical Jesus born of the Virgin Mary. He is Eternal Wisdom, joy and happiness of the Father in the Trinity, brilliant craftsperson of the cosmos and of all creation, but above all madly in love with human beings. Only this love could lead Wisdom to bring together what we are: our flesh, our weakness, our suffering and our death, so that we can become spouse of Wisdom herself, enter into her light, into her life, into her relationship with the Father. Montfort wants to be our guide and companion on the road as we discover and love Eternal Wisdom.

This document was submitted to a small team of Daughters of Wisdom and Friends of Wisdom from Canada who took the time to read it, identify mistakes, and make helpful suggestions.

## Steps

For each chapter (except chapters 10 and 11 which have been treated together as they develop the same theme), four elements are offered:

### 1. Discovery

This section aims to clarify or deepen one aspect or other of Montfort's thought developed in the chapter, sometimes also to enrich it especially from the Biblical aspect.

### 2. Difficulties to Overcome

You have to take into account that Montfort's text is not always easy. The images can surprise us, affirmations can even shock us. This section therefore seeks to overcome the difficulties in discovering the essence of the message. On the other hand, it aims also to clear the difficulties and obstacles that come from ourselves, our fears, our prejudices.

### 3. Development

In this section we will find questions and exercises, allowing us to grow in the knowledge of Christ-Wisdom and ourselves, to progress in the following of Montfort.

### 4. Prayer

Whether taking this spiritual journey alone or in a group, it is important to take time for prayer. The suggestions made here are a starting point. For several chapters, some stanzas from the "Canticles of Montfort" are suggested, which help us receive the same message in lyrical language.

## Advice that Divine Wisdom Gives to the Princes and the Great of the World

(Nos. 1-7)

### 1. Discovery

Montfort does not start by addressing the reader, but rather by addressing Wisdom. He begins by talking to Her because his goal is to get us to talk to Her, to meet Her, to be nourished by Her.

More than making us understand something; Montfort wants to set us out on the path to a treasure that he desires to share with us. Also, he uses paradox to make us grasp the important points of his subject:

- Gap between the greatness of Wisdom (*sovereign of heaven and earth*) and her proximity (*sitting at your door*);
- Contrast between the desire that exists in God for me and the absence of desire for God in me;
- The misfortune of those who invest their desire in the futile and in what is passing instead of concentrating it entirely on God.

## 2. Difficulties to Overcome

Montfort uses threatening language towards the rich and powerful. But, with Jesus, he does not want so much to condemn the rich and powerful as to warn them against the danger of accumulating possessions.

I look at myself: What do I long for: consumer goods? performance? hobbies?

## 3. Development

Montfort wants to lead me to the great discovery of his life: the love of Eternal Wisdom for him and for all human beings. I can only follow Her if I am docile. Docility is made of two things: trust in the one who guides me, and the humility to admit that I do not know everything and that I am not everything. With confidence, I set off.

## 4. Prayer

Say the prayer to Wisdom slowly (Nos. 1-2) in a spirit of humble confidence.

# Reading Guide: Chapter 1

## To Love And Seek After Divine Wisdom It Is Necessary to Know Her

(Nos. 8-14)

### 1. Discovery

Montfort's teaching is based on a fundamental anthropological process: we go from perception, to emotion, and finally to action. We start by perceiving (knowing and tasting); then we love what is known and desire it. Finally, we set off and we take steps to acquire it.

Montfort presents the three main qualities of Eternal Wisdom:

1. She is the noblest of sciences, that which makes it possible to discover "what are the riches and the glory of this mystery: Christ in your midst, the hope of glory" (Col 1:27). A science that encompasses everything, because Christ is the origin and the meaning of the cosmos and of all history, "the alpha and the omega, the beginning and the end" (Rev 21:6).

2. The most delightful knowledge. This makes it possible to qualify knowledge: it is not an abstract knowledge, fruit of an explanation, but of a concrete knowledge, fruit of experience.

3. The most necessary knowledge. In the Bible, "knowing" often means "coming into close contact, living in a relationship with." We can read for example that Adam and Cain "knew" their wives and that they became pregnant (Gn 4:17). Likewise, in the Gospel, to know God is to live a deep relationship with Him: "Everything was given to me by my Father. No one knows the Son except the Father, and no one knows the Father except the Son, and he to whom the Son is willing to reveal Him" (Mt 11:27).

## 2. Difficulties to Overcome

To compare Wisdom to "the Father's breasts" is an image that seems bizarre to us. It is found in other authors of the time. (Louis-François of Argentan, Francis de Sales ...). It is a way of emphasizing the maternal dimension of God (cf. Is 49:14-15).

## 3. Development

It happens in sports—hockey, football—that a clumsy player scores a goal in his own team's net! So it is not everything "to score goals." In my life, I may have achieved several goals that I had set for myself. But the most important "goal," the meeting of my God and Creator, have I really reached it? Like a good coach, it's towards this goal that Montfort wants to train me.

Notice that in No. 14, Montfort presents the plan of his work. It's a kind of game plan to get us to aim at and get to the point of it.

**4. Prayer**

Canticle 125

# Reading Guide: Chapter 2

## Eternal Wisdom's Origin and Excellence

(Nos. 15-30)

### 1. Discovery

IN ORDER to discover the wealth of Wisdom, Montfort makes us "pass through" three levels or dimensions:

1. First there is Eternal Wisdom, the Son of God, or the "Word," according to the vocabulary of the Gospel of John (1:1-18), or even the "Beloved Son" in the language of the synoptics and of Paul (Mt 3:17; Mk 1:11; Lk 20:13; Ep 1:6). Montfort plunges us into the heart of the Trinity and of the most intense relationship that is: that which has always existed and which will always exist between the Father and his beloved Son. Eternal life consists in entering it.

2. The Old Testament has no experience of this mystery of the Trinity, but it does know two kinds of Wisdom. The first is the Wisdom of God, which is like an emanation of God, an energy, a power by which God creates the world and manages it.

3. The Old Testament also speaks of a Wisdom which is in the human being. This one is very practical: it is a skill. Thus, the

Bible speaks of the Wisdom of goldsmiths, weavers and sailors (cf. Ex 31:3; 35:25-35; Ez 27:8; Ps 107:27). But the most important skill is knowing how to succeed in life, to discover its meaning and thus grow towards personal fulfilment. However, Montfort tells us, this Wisdom is not a book, but a person, Jesus Christ.

Montfort makes us cross through the three levels of Wisdom and unites them among themselves in a great movement of Incarnation: The Wisdom which is in God eternally emanates from Him to create the world and human beings, is incarnated in Him to reveal His true vocation and guide Him there. This is the interpretation that Montfort gives to the plant images of No. 25.

Both in Greek and Hebrew, "Wisdom" is feminine. She also has the attributes of a woman: wife, mother, the one who begets, feeds, guides.

**2. Difficulties to Overcome**

Number16: "Eternal Wisdom is the breath of God." This expression surprises us. The translation of *Le Maîstre de Sacy* used by Montfort is based on the *Vulgate* which is a Latin translation of the original Greek which uses the word "*atmis*" where "*atmosphere*" comes from. The author wants to emphasize that Wisdom comes directly from God, as steam comes directly from boiling water. Modern translations will rather translate as "effluvium" or "emanation."

**3. Development**

Do you have your laptop? Are you eagerly waiting for your texts? This shows the need in us to communicate. Well, this "need" has always existed in God: God wants to communicate, but more than by a simple text. By giving us His Son, Eternal Wisdom, God wants to give us all that God is.

- I realize this "need of God" to communicate.
- How can I respond to this need of God now?

**4. Prayer**

Canticle 126

## Reading Guide: Chapter 3

### The Wondrous Power of Divine Wisdom's Works in the Creation of the World and of Humankind

(Nos. 31-40)

### 1. Discovery

MONTFORT invites us to take a marvelous look at the entire creation. He himself loved nature and appreciated being able to retire to wooded areas. For him, nature was a book that spoke to him of God. (cf. Canticle 157). Not only poets and artists, but scientists are often amazed at creation. One discovers not only an inexhaustible beauty, but also an often hidden order. Think of the Fibonacci sequence that we find from the galaxies to our DNA, through the arrangement of the petals of a flower.

But for Montfort there is more. God did not create the world like a potter who would make a vase and then put it on sale! God created the world in order to enter into a relationship with the world. Creative Wisdom is not just a craftswoman: she is a mother. God created the world by His Word and He expects a word that responds to Him: that of the human being. Unfortunately, this word, this response to the love of God did not come. Since then, the world has been cut off, amputated, unable to reach its full accomplishment.

## 2. Difficulties to Overcome

Number 35: "You formed man so that he might have dominion over creatures" (Ws 9:2). This quote refers to the book of Genesis in which God said to the man and woman He had just created: "fill the earth and dominate it" (Gen 1:28). The Hebrew verb used here belongs to the royal vocabulary. The human being is created in the image of God. God delegates to humans the management and care of creation, like a king reigns to take good care of his people. The abuse of creation cannot rely on this verse from the Bible; rather, it stems from our habit of overconsumption.

Number 39: Through sin, "the human loses all the goods received." We find the punishment disproportionate: for having "bitten an apple," he is condemned to death! But if you look closely at the story, you discover this: the real sin is not to have bitten the apple (the Bible simply says "the fruit"). It is to have listened to the temptation: "is God really on your side?" By creating you, would He have deprived you of the essential: life? This is what is to be understood by the word of the serpent: "No, you will not die; but if you eat it, you will become like Gods" (Gen 3:4). At this time distrust of God and self-importance are born in the heart of the human being: "I don't need the other; I can manage myself, I am self-reliant."

Through original sin, “the human loses everything received.” According to the Bible, the human being is created perfect and loses everything because of sin. This scenario is in direct contrast to that of science whereby the human evolves from a primitive being, living a precarious existence, towards a superior being, capable of mastering its environment. In front of this apparent contradiction, it should be recalled here that the first chapters of Genesis are not historical. These are myths, that is to say stories that aim to tell the why of things: why the world exists, why there is suffering, why the human heart is capable of hatred, violence, exploitation, etc. The Bible affirms that the world is a gift from God and that God cannot be the source of evil. This comes from the very heart of the person: this is where the deceitful serpent lives, which puts us on false paths of happiness. Jesus will affirm it in the Gospel: “evil comes from within humans” (cf. Mk 7:20-23).

### 3. Development

- I pause before a nature landscape (a tree, a flower, the forest, an undergrowth, the sea, a starry sky, a mountain); I take time to contemplate; I let wonder arise in me.

- I discover or rediscover something that fascinates me about human beings: their capacity to create, their need to surpass themselves.... I think of people in whom this is shown.

• Finally, I look at evil in its various forms: war, murder, terrorism, exploitation of human beings, abuse of power. Cataclysm, illness, death....

• I recognize my smallness, my ignorance, a certain complicity with evil through my selfishness, my indifference....

• I pray Psalm 8, or another which touches me (138, 139).

**4. Prayer**

Canticle 157

## Reading Guide: Chapter 4

### Wisdom's Astonishing Kindness and Mercy toward Humankind before Her Incarnation

(Nos. 41-51)

### 1. Discovery

ON JANUARY 29, 2017, a fanatic sniper entered the Grand Mosque of Quebec, adjacent to the church of St. Foy, fired into the crowd, leaving six dead and eight injured, six of them seriously, leaving 17 orphaned children. Faced with this tragedy which unfortunately is not unique, three reactions were evident:

- *Amazement* in seeing a student of "normal" appearance make such a gesture, in one of the most peaceful cities of North America;
- *Outrage* at a hate crime, an attack on innocent people;
- The movement of deep *compassion* for the victims.

All things considered, Montfort shows us the same reactions in God to evil:

- *Amazement*: surprise in a world He created perfect, God sees the wrong. In the heart of the person he created in His image, hatred and wickedness show their hideous faces.

• *Indignation*: God is allergic to evil, He cannot tolerate it nor bear it. One thinks of the word of Jesus: "go far from me, you who do evil" (Lk 13:27).

• *Compassion*: Jesus, Eternal Wisdom made flesh, spent His life healing. To heal the body of course, but above all to heal the soul affected by evil: to the one who could not walk, He began by forgiving (Mk 2:5).

Montfort wants above all to make us understand that God has never abandoned human beings. He quotes at length chapter 10 of the book of Wisdom to show us, through *lectio divina*, that Eternal Wisdom accompanied them throughout history, until the day when She became flesh in time.

Number 51 is very important: by giving us an overview of the whole history of the patriarchs, Montfort showed us how Wisdom has helped all the righteous in the Old Testament, enlightening them in their choices, supporting them in their trials, accompanying them with the sweetness of Her friendship. Hence the question: but why should I also not welcome Her in my life? This is what he will encourage us to do in the next chapter.

**2. Difficulties to Overcome**

Number 43. "He sinned more out of weakness and ignorance than out of malice." Man and woman were seduced by Satan. Montfort takes up an idea already sketched out by St. Paul (cf. 2 Cor 11:3) and developed by the Fathers of the Church, including Irénée of Lyon.

**3. Development**

- I reread chapter 10 of the book of Wisdom in a modern translation to rediscover it.
- I look at my own life: can I see there moments when Wisdom showed me Her presence and compassion?

**4. Prayer**

Canticle 52

## Reading Guide: Chapter 5

### Eternal Wisdom's Amazing Excellence

(Nos. 52-63)

### 1. Discovery

THIS chapter is a real *lectio divina*, a meditative reading of the Bible, where Montfort lets himself be penetrated by the Word of God and tries to discover the meaning for him, personally.

He wants to give us the "taste" of Eternal Wisdom, Jesus Christ. This is why he wants us to discover in it the source of true knowledge. Not only the most important knowledge, but also the most extensive, deepest and most useful. Let's not forget that in the Bible, the one who speaks is the great King Solomon who seeks in Wisdom all the important skills to succeed in his mission as king. Likewise, Montfort suggests, with Wisdom I will have all the skills necessary to attain my destiny in this world and in the next.

Montfort does not quote the last three verses of chapter 8 of the Book of Wisdom, because he wants our attention to stop on verse 18: "I was going to seek her from all sides." Montfort's goal is not only to give us a taste for Wisdom, but to get us started.

## 2. Difficulties to Overcome

At the end of this work, Montfort will tell us that desire is the first means to obtain Eternal Wisdom. But already Montfort wants to give birth to desire in us, because only desire can lead us to the joyful gift of ourselves. "My God, if you exist, let me know you," repeated Charles de Foucauld incessantly in his desire to meet God.

We must not be afraid of our poverty: poverty of our desire, poverty of our love for God ... our poverty is the empty cradle where Wisdom will be born.

## 3. Development

- I reread chapter 8 of the book of Wisdom replacing "Wisdom" with "Jesus."

- I meditate on this phrase from Leonard Cohen: "There is a crack in everything, and it is through it that light enters."

## 4. Prayer

Canticle 103

## Reading Guide: Chapter 6

### Wisdom's Urgent Desire to Give Herself to Humankind

(Nos. 64-73)

### 1. Discovery

THE only goal that Montfort follows in writing this book is that the two desires meet: the desire of God for us and our desire for God.

The first is already learned. This is what he explains in this chapter. God wants us to exist and to live. It is the incredible message that resonates throughout the Bible. "He chose us in Christ before the foundation of the world ... He predestined us to be for him adopted children by Jesus Christ: according to the purpose of his will" (Eph 1:4-5). When we get away from him, God panics, gets angry, despairs and shouts to us: "I do not take pleasure in the death of one who dies: come back and live!" (Ez 18:32). Sometimes it is difficult to believe in this love in order to respond to it.

The Bible confronts us with two exiles: the exile of the human person far from God, out of paradise. And the exile of God far from the human person, out of God's desire and love. This is basically sin. And if we say that Christ "saves us from sin," it is not so much that He saves me from my little faults, but above all that in Him, the meeting between God and humans becomes possible: exile in Him is completed: God and us are at home in each other's arms.

## 2. Difficulties to Overcome

Faith is much more than believing in God: it is believing that He desires me. Montfort was overwhelmed by this awareness.

I reflect on my faith with honesty. Does it consist simply in believing in a distant absolute Being? Is it to obey God in order to keep myself healthy in return? Or do I really believe, deep down inside, that God ardently desires me? That He has been waiting for me since the beginning of the world.

## 3. Development

- I recognize the poverty of my faith. I read No. 216 of the "Treaty of the True Devotion" where Montfort describes the faith of Mary. Then, I ask the Virgin to share her faith with me, because the Holy Spirit, through the mouth of Elizabeth, says of her: "Blessed is she who believed" (Lk 1:45).

## 4. Prayer

Canticle 44

## Reading Guide: Chapter 7

### Choosing True Wisdom

(Nos. 74-89)

### 1. Discovery

MONTFORT now considers that after the journey he has made us do, we are ready to "elect" that is to say, to choose Wisdom. But beware: everything that shines is not gold: there are several false Wisdoms.

The different false Wisdoms that Montfort describes all arise from the same attitude: "I am the center of the world and everything exists for me. The comparison of the moon can be enlightening. Try to calculate the number of kilometers the moon has travelled since its existence! It has been on the move for 4.5 billion years. On each orbit, it travels 2,290,000 kilometers, multiplied by 12 for a year and then by 4.5 billion years. This page is not large enough to write the number! However, after these billions of kilometers travelled, the moon is still very close: we even walked on it. Why? Because it is a prisoner. Trapped in an orbit. The moon can move as much as it wants, it will never go far. All the false Wisdoms Montfort is talking about have one thing in common: it stems from the fact that we are so easily trapped in an orbit ... around ourselves.

The second element is the lie. No one wants to appear selfish or proud. So we are trying to "make up for" our little selfishness by virtue, or even—this is the big fashion today—behind the fundamental requirement of being yourself! Montfort invites us to great freedom: to be free of oneself to go to the Other, to tear ourselves away from the orbit of ME to discover more than ourselves.

**2. Difficulties to Overcome**

In No. 74, Montfort speaks of the "corrupt world." However, at the beginning of this writing, he extolled the beauty of creation in (Nos. 31-34). But for Montfort, the world has been shattered by sin and it will remain so until the end. It was not until Vatican Council II that the Church invited us to discover the beauty and the value of our contemporary world, despite its sufferings:

- The joys and the hopes, the sorrows and the anguishes of the people of this time, especially of the poor and of all those who suffer are also the joys and the hopes, the sorrows and the anguishes of the disciples of Christ. There is nothing truly human that does not resonate in their hearts (*Gaudium et spes, No. 1)*.

Each era—ours too—suffers from its spiritual and intellectual limits. The theology of Montfort had its share of limits, which should not prevent us from discovering the riches of its message.

## 3. Development

- In rereading the various false Wisdoms described by Montfort, what are the elements that I find in our modern society?
- Are there other kinds of "false Wisdom" in the world today?
- I could, as Montfort, write the "ten commandments" of the false Wisdoms of the world today.

## 4. Prayer

Psalm 139 (138)

# Reading Guide: Chapter 8

## The Splendid Effects That Eternal Wisdom Produces in the Souls of Those Who Possess Her

(Nos. 90-103)

### 1. Discovery

OFTEN parents are fearful when they see their children going to secondary school (or high school). Because they know that at this point, they lose some control over the child's relationships. Other people will enter their life and influence them for better or for worse ... any relationship, even the slightest serious one, stays with us, influences us. Montfort tells us that if we truly accept Eternal Wisdom, Her presence will be felt in our lives. She will live in us; it will influence our moods and our decisions. But luckily, it will be a beneficial relationship. How? He describes it in five points:

- Wisdom will give us intelligence and discernment. In life we have to make tough choices. Wisdom guides us in these choices. In life too, we will be faced with complex situations, where sometimes good and bad are mixed. Wisdom then gives us foresight and good judgment.

- Wisdom is the Word that inspired the prophets. And therefore, She will bring up for us the words we need to enlighten and guide others, to convince them to take the path of life and to avoid that which leads to death.

- To welcome Wisdom is to welcome a presence of friendship, that of God. A presence that fills us, so that the thousand little frustrations pass over us like water on the duck's back, because we will always be focused on the essentials. Whatever the ups and downs of life, our peace will be deep and will not be reached. Somehow, we will be rooted in Him who abides forever. Our roots being solid, our branches will be able to expand and withstand storms.

- Wisdom brings with it strength of mind, that strength which is called virtue.

- Finally, Wisdom invests us with enthusiasm; She makes us enterprising, proactive. As they say, with it, problems become challenges to be overcome.

**2. Difficulties to Overcome**

In Number 91, Montfort affirms that Wisdom works Her effects in us "in a manner so secret that the very soul does not notice it." She protects us from ourselves! Indeed, we are so tempted to center everything on ourselves, that we easily attribute to ourselves what is a pure gift from God. Even when we love, we sometimes look at each other in the process of loving and take pride in it, and we are caught up in this famous orbit that we have already talked about.

**3. Development**

- Montfort presents to us the five gifts or effects that wisdom brings us when we welcome Her into our life. At this point in my life, which of these five gifts seems to me the most important?

**4. Prayer**

Canticle 5

## Reading Guide: Chapter 9

### Eternal Wisdom's Incarnation and Earthly Life

(Nos. 104-116)

### 1. Discovery

WHAT Montfort does not say in this chapter reveals his intention as much as what he says. More than half of the text deals with the Incarnation and the role that Mary played in it. The rest of Jesus' life is treated briefly, and Montfort practically ignores His public life, devoting only five or six lines to it.

The intention of Montfort is similar to that of Luke in what are called the stories of the childhood of Jesus. In the first two chapters of his gospel, Luke somehow lays the foundations for the whole gospel. Everything is based on two characters: on the one hand a God who gives himself, the Emmanuel, the Incarnate Word. But God may well give himself for centuries, if there is no one to welcome Him perfectly, there will be no Gospel. Therefore, the second foundation of the Gospel is humanity that welcomes God. But humanity is an abstraction. God can only give himself to a human being of flesh and bone. A human being who is perfectly open to God and His plan for humanity, a human being who is perfectly receptive to God.

This is what Montfort tries to tell us in this chapter. If he speaks of the "torrents of grace" that surge over Mary, he wants us to understand that in her there finally appears a human being perfectly capable of welcoming God. The Incarnation brings together "winning conditions": total gift (Emmanuel) and perfect welcome (Mary).

If Mary has received from God this perfect capacity to welcome God, it is not so that she is above others, but is in the service of others. She is there to teach us the art of welcoming the Infinite into our condition as creatures.

### 2. Difficulties to Overcome

Montfort sometimes uses concrete language to speak of grace. He speaks of a "vessel of grace" (No. 35), or of going "to draw grace from the store" that is the heart of Jesus (Hymn 44, p.78). As if grace was something that can be measured and weighed like flour! Grace (*hesed*) in the Bible is a favorable disposition toward someone. Thus, God presents himself to Moses as "the merciful and benevolent God" (Ex 34:6). The angel Gabriel tells Mary that she has received God's favor (which has been translated as "full of grace"). Finally, grace is none other than God himself giving himself free of charge to us, without any merit on our part.

## 3. Development

• I reread the story of the annunciation. I underline what Mary is doing. What does this teach me about "the art of welcoming God" at the school of Mary?

## 4. Prayer

Canticle 64

## Reading Guide: Chapter 10

### Incarnate Wisdom's Charming Beauty and Inexpressible Sweetness

(Nos. 117-122) and

## Reading Guide: Chapter 11

### Incarnate Wisdom's Gentle Speech and Behavior

(Nos. 123-132)

AS THESE two chapters deal with the same theme, we will deal with them together.

### 1. Discovery

Sweetness—which he always associates with kindness, friendliness, humility—occupies an important place in Montfort's writings. It comes first from his spiritual tradition. The great Bérulle invites us to contemplate Christ because "his sweetness tends to make us sweet" (*Letters, Vol. 3*). We know from his biographers that Montfort had a hot character. But the contemplation of Christ—and no doubt also great efforts on his part—gave rise to a great attraction and a real practice of meekness as he discovered it in Jesus.

In these two chapters, Montfort presents the various aspects of sweetness of Christ: in His origin, in His name, in His face, in His words, but especially in His gestures or His behavior (all of chapter XI).

The sweetness of Wisdom that Montfort invites us to welcome and imitate in our life has nothing to do with certain softness.

We can break it down into five elements:

1. Nonviolence: to be gentle is to refuse to let oneself live and to be contaminated by the violence that others show us. We cannot denounce violence if it already lives in us. And the only way to get rid of it, is not to copy it, but to let it die in us.

2. Compassion: It is letting yourself be united to, touched by the misery of the other. This attitude is that of God himself, so marvelously illustrated in the parable of the prodigal son (Lk 15:11-32).

3. Primacy of the person: this is to make happiness and growth of the other the goal of all my words and actions. Suddenly, it is to refuse to reduce the other to an instrument for my own ends; the person is more important than success, pleasure, comfort.

4. Patience: consists in believing in others, in believing that they are capable of still growing, despite their failures.

5. Forgiveness: is to refuse to reduce the other to his/her fault to affirm that every human being is more than the harm they can do. It is opening a door to hope for them instead of locking them in their guilt.

Biographers give us several examples of the sweetness of Montfort. He himself, who spent hours at the confessional, said, "I would rather suffer in purgatory for having been too gentle on my penitents, than for having treated them with desperate severity."

**2. Difficulties to Overcome**

In Number 132, Montfort concludes his development on the sweetness of Eternal Wisdom by presenting a vision that one of the great spiritual masters of the 14th century, Henri de Suzo had of Her. What may explain this choice is that the vision demonstrates that Eternal Wisdom contains everything in Herself: the masculine and the feminine, height and depth, distance and proximity. Then comes the final invitation to give Her one's heart.

**3. Development**

- Reread in Luke the following three episodes: the sinner Zacchaeus (Lk 19:1-10); the widow of Naim (Lk 7:11-16), the bent woman

(Lk13:10-17). Discover how the sweetness of Jesus manifests itself in each one.

• In the five elements of sweetness described above, specify the one that is the most difficult for you to live today.

**4. Prayer**

Canticle 41

# Reading Guide: Chapter 12

## Incarnate Wisdom's Core Teachings: What We Must Believe and Do in Order to Be Saved

(Nos. 133-153)

### 1. Discovery

THE title sheds light on the content: "core teachings." "Core," that is to say that everything is not there, that choices have been made. "Teachings," which means brief and unique teachings. This excludes what is too long, such as parables, speeches, or overly-developed narratives. Therefore, one should be aware of the limited nature of this chapter. On the other hand, it has the advantage of making us discover that not only is Jesus a sage, but that He often expressed Himself in the manner of the sages of the Old Testament. These most often used the *māšāl* which is translated as a proverb or a wise saying, *i.e.*, advice or an observation expressed in a brief formula, often using parallelism, antithesis, and comparison.

To find our way more clearly in all these teachings, we can group them in different ways. Here they are, indicated by their numbers and classified into four categories:

| GOD ACTS | GOD GUIDES MY ACTION | | GOD PROMISES |
|---|---|---|---|
| | Towards Him | Towards my neighbor | |
| 2, 12, 16, 17, 30, 33, 47, 62 | 1, 2, 4, 7, 8, 9, 11, 12, 13, 15, 25, 28, 29, 32, 39, 57 | 3, 6, 13, 37, 42, 44, 49, 52, 55b, 56, 59 | 5, 10, 14, 18, 19, 21, 22, 23, 24, 41, 45, 61 |

### 2. Difficulties to Overcome

Do you think TV commercials are exaggerated? This is normal: their goal is to hold our attention and lead us to take action: Buy! It is the same with the literary genre "*māšāl*" or proverb, used by the sages of the Bible, including Jesus. The proverb must capture our imagination with a strong image, a paradox, or a well-founded comparison. They should not be interpreted literally, but rather get the message out. For example, Jesus tells us to "present the other cheek if someone strikes us" (Mt 5:39); but He himself did not do so when He was attacked during His trial (Jn 18:22-23)! So through the picture, you get the message.

### 3. Development

- I reread the oracles by category, according to the table above. For each, I choose the oracle which gets my attention, and the oracle which I find the most difficult to accept or to accomplish.

### 4. Prayer

Psalm 23 (22)

## Reading Guide: Chapter 13

### The Sorrows That Incarnate Wisdom Chose to Undergo on Our Behalf

(Nos. 154-166)

### 1. Discovery

IN NUMBERS 154 to 162, Montfort describes different aspects of the cross or the suffering of Christ. It is striking that in this presentation, barely 20% of the text deals with his physical suffering during the passion! In this way, Montfort helps us to discover that Jesus did not only suffer the three hours that He was on the cross! Little is known of the first thirty years of Jesus' life, but we know that from the start of His ministry, He was attacked from all sides. Suspicions, mockery, refusals, and condemnations are piling up. It can be said that suffering became a part of Jesus very early in His public life. From the beginning of chapter 3 of his gospel, Mark teaches us that "the Pharisees went out and began to plot with the Herodians how they might kill Jesus" (Mk 3:6). Similarly in the second chapter of the Gospel of John, He is faced with incomprehension (Jn 2:18-21), and in chapter 5, one begins to see His death plot (Jn 5:18). Finally, let us remember that the three synoptic gospels report that Jesus was rejected by His own kin (Mk 6:1-6; Mt 13:54-58; Lk 4:16-30). Therefore, when Jesus invites His disciples to "take up their cross," it means to accept everything that makes them suffer: annoyances, conflicts, pettiness, injustices, stress, and discomfort. In short, everything that hurts us in one way or another.

### 2. Difficulties to Overcome

Montfort's insistence on suffering makes many uncomfortable. Did he have a kind of morbid attraction for suffering?

Here are some of the explanations:

First, in his own life experience. Throughout most of his life, his vitality, a certain awkwardness in his relations with others (which he will admit to his friend Blain), and the radical aspect of his relationship to God brought him rejections, mockery, slander, and persecution. Three years before his death, he wrote to his sister:

> If you knew half of the crosses and humiliations I have to bear, I don't think you would be eager to see me.... I have always to be on the alert, treading warily as though on thorns or sharp stones. I am like a ball in a game of tennis; no sooner am I hurled to one side than I am sent back to the other, and the players strike me hard. This is the fate of a poor sinner. I have been without

> rest or respite all of the thirteen years since leaving Saint-Sulpice (Letter 26).

Montfort saw his projects thwarted by the jealousy or inertia of others. Twice he was dismissed from Poitiers general hospital. His reputation was tarnished by slander which led to him being banned from ministry in seven dioceses. In Pontchâteau, he experienced his great Calvary—a project he dreamed of for years—demolished.

Human beings have a deep need to find meaning in their life and especially in their suffering. Often in the media, we hear that parents whose child has died from an "unknown" disease are launching a foundation for medical research, declaring: "I do not want my child to die for nothing!" It is in the Cross of Christ that Montfort discovers not only the meaning, but the mysterious fruitfulness of his personal suffering. In the letter quoted above, after speaking of interior joy that accompanies his suffering, he says:

> There is great merit from carrying crosses. I wish you could see mine. I have never had more conversions than after the most painful and unjust experiences.

Finally, Montfort never suffered from a kind of masochism that made him look for suffering. He writes in his *Letter to the friends of the cross*:

Do not deliberately contrive to bring crosses upon yourself. We must not do what is wrong in order to bring about something good, nor must we without the inspiration of God do things badly so as to draw down ridicule on yourself. Rather, we ought to imitate Jesus Christ, who is said to have done all things well, not out of pride or vanity, but to please God and to win over His neighbor. And if you fulfil your duties as well as you can, you will find no lack of opposition, criticism and ridicule, which will be sent by divine Providence without your choosing or wanting it (No. 42).

### 3. Development

- On a sheet of paper, I draw two columns. In the first, I note the challenges that I lived in my life: suffering in my relationships with others, in my work, in my body through illness, in my spiritual life ... in the second column, I note what positive effects these sufferings have had in my human, spiritual, relational growth.

### 4. Prayer

Canticle 19

# Reading Guide: Chapter 14

## Eternal Wisdom's Triumph in and by the Cross

(Nos. 167-180)

### 1. Discovery

THE Cross is at the heart of our faith. Saint Paul affirms it throughout his epistles:

"But we preach a crucified Messiah, scandal for the Jews, foolishness for the pagans" (1 Cor 1:23). "When I came to you, brethren, it was not with the prestige of words or wisdom that I came to announce the mystery of God to you. For I have decided not to know anything among you, except Jesus Christ, and Jesus Christ crucified "(1Cor 2:1-2). "For me, no, never any other title of glory than the cross of our Lord Jesus Christ; by it, the world is crucified for me, as I for the world" (Ga 6:14).

But this Cross is a mystery. In his beautiful book on Wisdom in the New Testament, N.T. Wright comments on the quotes from 1 Corinthians:

> One of the reasons why the gospel mystery is a mystery is that no one in Corinth or elsewhere would have thought of looking for the secret of life, the universe, God, beauty, love and death at a place of execution, at the gates of a rebel city in the Near

> East! In the ancient world, the crucifixion was considered to be such a horrible, revolting and degrading thing that it was not even mentioned in good society. (...) But Paul believed that it was the key to the mystery of life (*New Testament Wisdom for Everyone*, SPCK, London, 2013, p. 5).

In the person of Jesus, a new, powerful world has burst into our earth: the very world of God! But this power is revealed in the non-power of the Cross. To properly unmask the powers based on the force of arms, money, prestige, it was necessary that real power be manifested in the nudity of the Cross. "The Cross is a very deep mystery here below" sang Montfort (Canticle 19, 1). N. T. Wright joined him, saying:

> [In Christianity,] there is a treasure of knowledge, of understanding of life waiting to be explored. It is not just a set of beliefs or a manual of directives for life that one could read and master over a weekend. It is as complex as the universe, full of beauty, mystery, power, also terrifying and wonderful as God himself. There is always so much more to understand and savor (see p. 7).

Let's not be afraid to dive into the mystery of the Cross: it leads us to the mystery of God and man; it makes us drink from the secret sources of life, as the poet Félix Leclerc wrote:

- Death is crazy, meaner than the wind.
- Death is deaf, like a dead man on a bench.
- Death is black and laughs.
- Death is great, it is full of life (*life, love, death*).

1. Difficulties to Overcome

*A strange exegesis*

First recognize that the exegesis of Montfort in this chapter is a bit confusing. Indeed, by quoting out of context, he applies biblical passages to the Cross which have a completely different meaning. For example, in No. 169, he quotes: "I loved her from my youth," but this passage expresses the love of Solomon for Wisdom... in No. 170, he quotes the word of Christ at the Last Supper: "I desired with an infinite desire," as if Jesus expressed his desire to suffer on the cross. But the full text is: "I wanted so much to eat this Passover with you before I suffered" (Lk 2:15). To say that Jesus "sought [the Cross] with unspeakable joy" (No. 170) is a pious exaggeration when we know that the Gospel tells us rather than in agony he prayed that the cup of suffering be taken away from him and he is overcome with anguish (Lk 22:42-44).

*Absence of the resurrection*

The absence of references to the resurrection of Christ in this writing of Montfort is striking. The word "resurrection" does not appear anywhere, and the verb "to resuscitate" applied to Christ appears only to tell us that it happened on April 5 (No. 116)! Montfort ignores the many passages where Paul develops his thought on the resurrection of Christ and ours.

This is all the more surprising since the Gospels tell us that we cannot understand the Cross of Christ without the resurrection! When he recounts the mysterious words of Jesus comparing himself to the temple, the evangelist explains: "When Jesus rose from the dead, his disciples remembered that he had spoken thus, and they believed in the writing as well as in the word which he had spoken" (Jn 2:22). Let us also mention Lk 18:34; Mt 16:21-23; Mk 9:31; Lk 24:6-8. Finally, let us remember that for Paul, the heart of the profession of faith relates to the resurrection of Christ: "if from your mouth, you confess that Jesus is Lord and if in your heart, you believe that God raised him from the dead, you will be saved" (Rom 10:9).

This absence of the resurrection can be explained in two ways. Montfort's Christology is a restorative Christology: Jesus is God, His death is therefore a sacrifice of infinite value which erases our sins, wrestles us from the clutches of the devil to which we belong by our sins and opens the door to heaven. One could perhaps say that for Montfort, the saving work of Christ is completed on the Cross: the resurrection is only the last miracle which comes to confirm His divinity. The transformative aspect of salvation is not very present in the theology that Montfort received. Christ does not appear very much like humanity already transformed, "the first born of a multitude of brothers" (Rom 8:29), who are transformed in his image, day after day in the power of the spirit.

However, there is an eschatological tension in Montfort, which is expressed, if one can discreetly say, in the language of "fullness," a word which occurs ten times under his pen in this work. This links him with the magnificent developments of Saint Paul on the pleroma (Ep 4:13; Col 2:2) and the theme of achievement *(teleios)* so present in the New Testament (He 5:9; 7:11; Jn 17:23; 1 Jn 2:5; Ph 3:12).

Finally, let us mention that Montfort does not aim here to explain to us the process by which Jesus saves us. Its purpose is not so much to explain as to make us discover the immense love of Christ for each of us personally, love which was manifested in the gift of His life on the Cross. In doing so, Montfort wants to bring us to respond to this love by the total gift of self. We cannot offer crumbs to the one who gave everything.

*What to do with his suffering?*

This is what Montfort is coming to. We all have our "piece of the cross," our share of suffering. What do we do with it? What does it give birth to in us? Despair? Revolt? Anxiety? Contemplating the cross of Christ, Montfort made a great discovery: Jesus took what is most ugly in the human condition—suffering—and made it the most beautiful: love! Dare we make a somewhat lame comparison? You are caught with your table scraps; you have to pay to get rid of them. Someone arrives who says to you: "but this waste is recyclable; it's gold: you can make great compost from it." Montfort repeats four times in No. 176: "The cross is good. It is good, if I dare say it, because it is "recyclable," because we can make something very precious of it, because, with Christ and in Christ, we can transform it into something beautiful, something that brings salvation. The cross without Christ hurts; the cross in Christ heals."

**3. Development**

• I slowly re-read Phil 2, 6-11. I pray to Christ, humbly asking him to make me enter more deeply into the mystery of his death and resurrection.

• I reread No. 176 by replacing "the cross" with "my cross." Then I come back to this reading to see what it brought me to.

**4. Prayer:**

Canticle 11

## Reading Guide: Chapter 15

### Two Means to Obtain Divine Wisdom: Ardent Desire and Continuous Prayer

(Nos. 181-193)

### 1. Discovery

IT IS not for nothing that Montfort puts in the same chapter the first two means of obtaining Wisdom: desire and prayer. They are intimately linked.

*Desire*

For Buddhism and some schools of philosophy, desire is the source of suffering. Indeed, if one does not obtain the object of one's desire, one suffers. Christianity has a paradoxical vision of desire which can be summed up in the axiom: "We must expect nothing and desire everything." This means that you should avoid investing your desire in the trivial, the superficial, and the transient. Human desire is infinite and therefore only the Infinite can fulfill it. So you should expect nothing transient (good weather, a beautiful house, impeccable health), but desire everything, that is to say desire everything that is God, or for Montfort, Eternal Wisdom.

*Prayer*

Prayer is the expression of this desire for God and before God. To pray is to stand before the Infinite while being aware of one's own nothingness, of its radical poverty. It is to stand before God in truth and trust. The truth: "What have you not received?" (1 Cor 4:7). This is the truth of my earthly state. And confidence: "If you, who are bad know how to give good things to your children, how much more will your Heavenly Father ..." (Lk 11:13). Montfort says that prayer must be continual. One should aim, ideally, to always be in a "state of prayer," that is to say, the heart turned toward God, listening to Him. Because, the goal and the summit of prayer is that the two desires meet: the immense desire of God to give Himself to the world (what Jesus calls the kingdom of God) and the immense desire of the human being to let themselves be penetrated and guided by this desire. Perfect prayer is summed up in the Our Father, where we only ask one thing of God: it is to be perfectly attuned to His plan ("your will, your reign") so that it will be realized in us and through us, as it was realized in Jesus and through Him.

Solomon's prayer shows us that we are not asking God to give us Wisdom once and for all. This is not an object, but a life companion, who enlightens us in our choices and makes us strong in our difficulties.

## 2. Difficulties to Overcome

Montfort warns us against the attraction of the marvelous and the sensitive in our relationship with God. Not only does it risk focusing on ourselves, but also imagining that God is reduced to pleasant emotions. God is beyond everything, the Elusive. And God is free to give Himself when and as He wants. This is why the first quality of prayer is not fervor, but constancy! Moreover, it is not so in our human relationships: the most solid are not the most "burning," but those whose consistency reveals depth. Prayer is like the long work of the tree which plunges its roots ever deeper. So my prayer is rooted in the depth of the two desires.

## 3. Development

This is a good opportunity to reflect on my prayer life:

- How has my prayer changed over the years? What obstacles have I encountered? What helped me to overcome them? From what deep desire is my prayer born?

- What importance do I attach to prayer? Is it daily, constant? If I pray less than before, how did I get there? What means can I take to deepen my prayer?

## 4. Prayer

Canticle 124

## Reading Guide: Chapter 16

### The Third Means to Obtain Divine Wisdom: Universal Mortification

(Nos. 194-202)

1. **Discovery**

WE sometimes notice people around us who attract our admiration and respect. It gives them depth, confidence, a sense of order and meaning. Where does it come from? Most of the time, these people have made a radical choice in their lives, around which their other choices are organized. "Radical" comes from root. This evokes the image of a tree with deep, solid roots, which ensure and nourish the growth of the trunk, branches, leaves and fruits. These "tree-people" are far from the legendary weather vane which does not know on which side it will turn, because it is the wind which decides… two dangers lie in wait for us: either we never make a choice and let others decide, or make the wrong choice.

> Do not conform to the present age, but be transformed by the renewal of your intelligence to discern what the will of God is: what is good, what pleases him, what is perfect (Rom 12:2, Ecumenical translation).

In the work already cited, N.T. Wright sheds light on the meaning of this verse quoted by Montfort in No. 198.

Like many Jews of his time, Paul believed that the history of the world was divided in two: on the one hand, "the present age" characterized by the revolt against God with the corruption and death which results from it; on the other hand, "the age to come" where God will give new life to the world and to humanity, bringing justice, joy, peace once and for all. An important element of Paul's gospel is to believe that "the age to come" has already occurred in Jesus, and most prominently in His death and resurrection (Wright, op. cit., p. 22).

Consequently, the two "ages" coexist; the Christian, in a way has both feet in them and must constantly choose which one he wants to belong to. This is why Paul says that we must be "transformed" in our way of thinking to avoid basing our choices on the old world, source of violence and suffering, and to choose the new world, source of life and peace. This does not mean that the Christian despises the world and the society in which he lives. But he is aware that this world is affected by a deep evil that needs to be healed. He is also aware that, as he is immersed in this world, he can very well, without realizing it, be seduced by its values and adjust his choices. Much like the citizens of a city with a polluted atmosphere no longer realize the poison they swallow with each breath.

### 2. Difficulties to Overcome

We can criticize Montfort for having a negative vision of the world. In this he was a man of his time. But we must recognize his great insights. Through these, he knew how to discern the hypocrisy and the lie of his time. He saw how easy it is for humans to be seduced by the futile and to pursue what the "world" believes: success, money, pleasure.

There is a certain progression in the thought of Montfort: he warns us against "the goods," then "the modes" and finally "the maxims"—which are more interior and can distort our whole vision of life and guide our choices.

The idea of "mortifying your body" is the very opposite of our society that glorifies the body. But we just have to think of all forms of "dependence" to understand what Montfort was aiming at. Addictions to food, alcohol, drugs, cell phones, TV or the internet: they all take away our freedom.

### 3. Development

• Looking at my life, I look at the important choices I have made. On what were they based: on "the present age" or on "the coming age" inaugurated in the person of Christ?

• I look at my small daily choices and I ask myself the same question about them to become aware of the subtle addictions that have seeped into my life.

### 4. Prayer

Psalm 1

## Reading Guide: Chapter 17

### The Fourth Means to Obtain Divine Wisdom: True Devotion to the Blessed Virgin Mary

(Nos. 203-222)

### 1. Discovery

THIS last chapter of Montfort contains very few references to the Gospels: a quote from Lk 1:42 and a reference to Lk 2:19, about Mary "who kept these events in her heart (or "these words"). There is also no quotation or even specific reference to any spiritual author. Does this indicate that Montfort shares with us here, above all, his own experience, both personally and pastorally?

In the passages of the Gospel which speak to us about Mary, we can perceive a certain tension. On the one hand, her maternal relationship to Christ is put on the back burner:

- At the age of twelve, Jesus affirms that His fundamental relationship is not with His parents, but with His Father (Lk 2:49).

- When told that his mother and brothers are looking for Him, Jesus answers:

- "Who are my mother and my brothers?" And looking around at those who sat in a circle around him, he said: "Here is my mother and my brothers: Whoever does the will of God is my brother, my sister, my mother" (Mk 3:31-35).

• In Cana, when Mary reports the lack of wine, Jesus addresses her as He does to other women, calling her "Woman" (cf. Jn 4:21; 8:10). Then he continues: "What do you want from me? My hour has not yet come" (Jn 2:4).

• Finally, when a woman in the crowd exclaims: "Blessed is the womb that carried you and the breasts that you sucked" (literal translation), Jesus replies: "Blessed are those who listen to the word of God and who observe it." (Lk 11:27-28). This is the last reference to Mary in the Gospel of Luke.

But on the other hand, Mary is introduced to us as very close to her Son:

• At the Annunciation, she declares the gift of her being to God: "I am the servant (literally "the slave") of the Lord; let it happen to you according to your word" (Lk 1:38).

• Then, through the mouth of Elizabeth, the Holy Spirit proclaims a double blessing: that of the mother and the son (Lk 1:42) and attributes to Mary the first of the Beatitudes of the Gospel: "Blessed is she who has believed: what has been said to her from the Lord will be fulfilled" (Lk 1:45).

- Mary's thanksgiving prayer then arises when she declares: "All generations will proclaim me blessed, because the Almighty has done great things for me."

- The Magi will find the child in his mother's arms, and thereafter, Matthew always names them together (Mt 2:11; 13-14; 20-21).

- At the temple, Simeon prophesies that the destinies of Jesus and of Mary are linked and that she will suffer because of it (Lk 2:34-35).

- In Cana, Mary declares: "Do whatever he tells you": this is the very response of the people entering into an alliance with God (cf. Ex 19:8; 24:3).

- Mary, first and perfect disciple, gives birth to faith in the hearts of the other disciples: "Jesus manifested his glory and his disciples believed in him" (Jn 2:11).

- Finally, at the foot of the cross, Jesus founds His new family, based not on blood, but on faith (Jn 19:25-27).

From this we can conclude: Mary is inseparable from her Son, more by her discipleship than by the biological link. She is united to her life and her work. She was called to a unique way of being a disciple of Christ by also being His mother. His role, as at Cana, is to teach us to welcome the Word in all that we are and to follow it throughout our lives.

## 2. Difficulties to Overcome

Montfort presents Mary as the fourth means of acquiring Wisdom. But by giving so much importance to what is for him "the greatest of means," does it not seem almost to eliminate the other means? On the contrary! They are not eliminated but taken over, since she lived them to perfection. Montfort invites us to insert our desire, our prayer, our mortification into the desire, prayer and mortification of Mary, so that with her and in her, they will be brought to their perfection.

Montfort explains to us that Mary is "the mother, mistress and throne" of Divine Wisdom. We understand that she is the mother of Jesus. But the mistress? She who declared herself "the slave" (Lk 1:38)? Montfort tries to make us understand that the bond, the communion between Christ and Mary is so deep, that Mary wants everything that Christ wants and vice versa. And how is she the "throne"? A throne—or any official seat—reveals the function and status of the person who sits there. Thus, Mary is the "throne of Christ" because she is so inhabited by Christ that, in all that she is and does, she reveals Christ to us, as a prism reveals the color of light.

### 3. Development

- Read the two passages from Saint John that tell us about Mary: the wedding of Cana (Jn 2:1-12) and the last words of Jesus addressed to the disciples (Jn 19:25-27).

### 2. Prayer

Canticle 155

## Consecration to Jesus Christ, Incarnate Wisdom, through the Hands of Mary
(Nos. 223-227)

### 1. Discovery

THE text of the consecration holds a great mystical breath. It is also animated by a movement which goes from contemplation to commitment.

*O Eternal and Incarnate Wisdom*

Is a movement of contemplation of Wisdom in the three relationships that give it its identity: relationship to its Father, relationship to Mary, relationship to us, sinners.

*But unfortunately! Ungrateful and unfaithful that I am*

A conversion movement: awareness of our state: what we have done or not done has seriously affected our relationship with God.

*This is why I have recourse... I salute you, oh Mary...*

Mary is "younger than sin"; (G. Bernanos) in her, there is no resistance, no indifference to God, but the total and loving gift of her being. She is the creature most intimately linked to the work of salvation of Christ. So I turn to her to help me get in touch with Him and live.

*I, an unfaithful sinner, renew in your hands the vows of my baptism.*

No one can baptize themselves. We *receive* baptism, it's a gift. To baptize means to "plunge." Through baptism, I am immersed in the total and eternal "yes" of the Father to His Son and of the Son to His Father, both in eternity and in His incarnation. To be baptized is therefore also to adhere to the "yes" of Christ in time, in our flesh, in all our choices.

*I choose you for my mother and mistress...*

The whole being of Mary belongs to Christ. I give myself to her, so that with her and in her, I may belong as completely as possible to Christ.

*O admirable Mother, mother of mercy, Faithful Virgin…*

The triple prayer to the Virgin so that she sets out on the road with us, that she be our companion throughout our journey on earth, in order to participate in the "fullness" of Christ, the Son loved by the Father and Mary.

**2. Difficulties to Overcome**

The term "slave" evokes in us the horrors of slavery in the West, especially in the South of the United States. Moreover, in our society, autonomy is a sign of maturity: I decide for my life; I make my choices. So why this term? Montfort does not aim to evoke submission to a master, but rather total belonging to another, and a belonging to love. Therefore, a total and free gift of self out of love. A bit like we see a mother giving herself to her children (her time, her energies, her resources belong to them) or an adult son or daughter devoting themselves to sick or disabled parents.

### 3. Development

- In his *Treatise on the True Devotion* (Nos. 227-232), Montfort offers a process of preparation for this act of consecration. Reading *The Love of Eternal Wisdom*, along with the approach proposed in this Reading Guide, can be a good preparation for consecration. When possible, it's best to do it with others, in a celebration where everyone signs their dedication form.

### 4. Prayer

Canticle 77

## Prayers of St. Louis-Marie de Montfort

### Prayer for the Spirit of Mary

MY POWERFUL Queen,
you are all mine through your mercy,
and I am all yours.
Take away from me all that may displease God
and cultivate in me all that is pleasing to Him.
May the light of your faith
dispel the darkness of my mind,
your deep humility
take the place of my pride,
your continual sight of God
fill my memory with His presence;
may the fire of the charity of your heart
inflame the lukewarmness of my own heart;
may your virtues take the place of my sins;
may your merits be my enrichment
and make up for all
that is wanting in me before God.

My beloved Mother,
grant that I may have no other spirit but your spirit,
to know Jesus Christ and His Divine Will
and to praise and glorify the Lord,
that I may love God with burning love like yours.

## Prayer for the Church of God

O LORD,
remember Your Church.
You possessed her in Your mind from all eternity,
thinking of her from the beginning.
You possessed her in Your hands
when You created the universe out of nothing
at the beginning.

You possessed her in Your heart
when Your dear Son died on the Cross
and watered her with His Blood
and consecrated her by His Death,
entrusting her to His holy Mother.

Heed, O Lord,
the designs of Your mercy.
Raise up new workers from Your right hand,
as You have done in the past,
in giving prophetic qualities
to some of Your greatest servants:
give us another St. Francis de Paul, St. Vincent Ferrer,
or St. Catherine of Siena.

## Words of
## St. Louis-Marie de Montfort

### About the Blessed Mother

The salvation of the whole world began with the "Hail Mary."

Hence, the salvation of each person is also attached to this prayer.

You never think of Mary without Mary thinking of God on your behalf.

Neither do you ever praise and honor God without Mary praising and honoring God in union with you.

During her earthly life Mary lived in continual prayer.

Therefore, all who are devoted to her must pray—and pray continually.

Mary is the living "mold of God." It was in her that God was made a true man.

It is also in her that human beings can be truly fashioned into God, insofar as that is possible for human nature, by the grace of Christ.

In the interior life and in the apostolate, let us always work with Mary.

For then everything becomes easier and more certain, quicker and more delightful.

Nowhere do we find Jesus nearer to us and more adapted to our weakness than in Mary, since it was for that reason that He came and dwelt in her.

Everywhere else He is the Bread of the strong, the Bread of the Angels, but in Mary He is the Bread of children.

Mary is my great treasure. She is my All after Jesus.

She is my honor, my tenderness, and the storehouse of my virtues! I do everything in and through her.

The Blessed Virgin will give you a share of her faith, a faith that will remove all concern with sensible and extraordinary things.

This faith will be living and animated by love so that you will act entirely out of love.

Mary's prayers and requests are so powerful with God that they pass for commands with His Majesty.

He never resists the prayer of His dear Mother because it is always humble and in accord with His will.

To go to Jesus through Mary is truly to honor Jesus Christ.

It indicates that we do not esteem ourselves worthy of approaching His infinite holiness directly, that we need Mary to be our Mediatrix with Him, our Mediator.

Rising or going to bed, leaving or returning, away or at home, I have the "Hail Mary" always on my lips. I am insuperable when I say it.

To become perfect, say a Rosary a day.

Mary imparts to her children both their crosses and the grace to carry them patiently and even cheerfully.

Thus it is that the crosses she lays upon those who belong to her are steeped in sweetness rather than filled with bitterness.

## The Life of St. Louis-Marie de Montfort

April 28

LOUIS Mary Grignion was born to a poor family on January 21, 1673, at Montfort, France. He was educated at the Jesuit college in Rennes and was ordained there in 1700. He was assigned as chaplain to a hospital at Poitiers, and his much needed reorganization of the hospital staff caused great resentment, leading to his resignation. However, during his stay there he organized a group of women into the congregation of the Daughters of Divine Wisdom.

Eventually Louis went to Rome where Pope Clement XI appointed him missionary apostolic, and he began to preach in Britanny. His emotional style caused much reaction, but he was successful, especially in furthering devotion to the Blessed Virgin through the Rosary. He also wrote a popular book, *True Devotion to the Blessed Virgin*, which has become a classic.

In 1715, Louis organized several priests and formed the Missionaries of the Company of Mary. He died in 1716 at Saint-Laurent-sur Sèvre, France, and was canonized in 1947 by Pope Pius XII.

## Prayer

*God, You willed to direct the footsteps of St. Louis, Your Priest, in the way of salvation and the love of Christ, with the accompaniment of the Blessed Virgin. Grant that following his example we may meditate on the mysteries of Your love and strive indefatigably to build up Your Church. Amen.*

# OTHER OUTSTANDING CATHOLIC BOOKS

**EVERY DAY IS A GIFT**—Introduction by Rev. Frederick Schroeder. Short, popular meditations for every day, featuring a text from Sacred Scripture, a timeless quotation from the writings of a Saint, and a meaningful prayer. Printed in two colors. **No. 195**

---

**ST. JOSEPH SUNDAY MISSAL**—The complete Masses for Sundays, Holydays, and the Sacred Paschal Triduum. Includes the Readings for the 3-year Cycle (A, B, and C) and Mass texts in accord with *The Roman Missal,* Third Edition. **No. 820**

---

**CHRISTIAN PRAYER**—The official one-volume edition of the internationally acclaimed *Liturgy of the Hours.* This version contains the complete texts of Morning and Evening Prayer for the entire year. The large type is ideal for those with difficulty in reading. **No. 406**

---

**CATHOLIC BOOK OF PRAYERS**—GIANT TYPE EDITION. Rev. Maurus FitzGerald, O.F.M. Today's most popular general prayer book. Contains many favorite prayers—for every day, to the Blessed Trinity, to Mary, and to the Saints, as well as a summary of our Faith. **No. 910**

---

**THE IMITATION OF CHRIST**—GIANT TYPE EDITION. This treasured book has brought peace to readers for many ages by showing how to follow the life of Christ to which all are called. **No. 322**

---

**THE IMITATION OF CHRIST (Abridged Edition)**—Adapted by Sr. Halcon J. Fisk. This classic work on the spiritual life is adapted for contemporary readers. Contains the essence of Thomas à Kempis's masterpiece in digestible form. **No. 362**

---

**INTRODUCTION TO A DEVOUT LIFE**—Adapted by Sr. Halcon J. Fisk. St. Francis de Sales, known as the apostle of love, reached out to everyone through this small book, showing that devotion is available to everyone in every walk of life and occupation. **No. 163**

---

**THE IMITATION OF MARY**—By Rev. Alexander de Rouville, S.J. Modern version of the companion volume to *The Imitation of Christ.* The author follows the Blessed Virgin through the different mysteries and circumstances of her life. Contains full-color inserts. **No. 330**

---

**TREASURY OF NOVENAS**—By Rev. Lawrence G. Lovasik, S.V.D. More than forty popular Novenas carefully arranged for private prayer in accord with the Liturgical Year on the Feasts of Jesus, Mary, and favorite Saints. With full-color inserts and Dura-Lux cover. **No. 345**

---

**catholicbookpublishing.com**

See more titles now.

ISBN 978-1-953152-99-2
90000
9 781953 152992